Battling Spiritual Warfare

Allen Linn

Copyright © 2018 by Allen Linn

1314 Grandview Circle
Buffalo, MN 55313
763-486-2867
www.pyramidpublishers.com

All rights reserved. No part of this publication may be reproduced, stored in a retrieval system, or transmitted, in any form or by any means, electronic, mechanical, photocopying, recording, or otherwise, without the prior written permission of the author.

Printed by Lightning Source
1246 Heil Quaker Blvd.
La Vergne, TN USA 37086
ISBN – 978-0-9982014-5-0

Cover Design by Dreamstime and Elaine Lanmon
Interior by Just Ink Digital
Printed in the United States of America

Unless otherwise noted, Scripture quotations are from The Holy Bible, New International Version™, NIV™, Copyright© 1973, 1978, 1984, 2011 by Biblica, Inc.™ Used by permission of Zondervan

TABLE OF CONTENTS

Chapter	Page
Introduction Spiritual Warfare	4
1 Lucifer's Creation and Fall	8
2 Mankind's Creation and Fall	11
3 Mankind's Fall and the Promised Redeemer.	21
4 Satan's Defeat at the Cross	31
5 Born to Battle	39
6 God's Full Armor	45
7 God's Full Armor 2	54
8 The Devil's Names and Titles and His Character	65
9 The Devil's Power and Influence and Methods	70
10 The World	80
11 The Flesh	87
12 The Good Angels	91
13 Prayer	99

INTRODUCTION
SPIRITUAL WARFARE

Angels are referred to almost 300 times in the Bible. They are a prominent part of God's program for mankind. The Word "angel" in both the Old Testament Hebrew and New Testament Greek means "messenger." They are revealed in the Bible as an order of supernatural spirit beings, of which there are different classes and rankings.

Some believe that the "sons of God" in Genesis 6:2 refers to angels, but the Bible is clear that angels are non-material. They are called "ministering spirits" in Hebrews 1:14. They do not possess physical bodies, although good angels may take on physical bodies when God appoints them to special duties. We never read of bad angels taking on physical bodies. Instead, they seek to enter into human beings and possess them. Furthermore, they do not reproduce.

Genesis 6:2 refers to godly men marrying ungodly women. Satan was seeking to corrupt the godly line. Their offspring were the Nephilim, the heroes of old, men of renown, men who made a reputation for themselves for violence and iniquity. Nimrod was such a man, who grew to be a mighty warrior on the earth. He is described as being "a mighty hunter before the Lord." The first centers of his kingdom were Babylon, Erech, Akkad, and Culneh, in Shinar. "From that land he went to Assyria, where he built Nineveh, Rehoboth Ir, Calah, and Resen, which is between Nineveh and Culneh; that is the great city" (Genesis 10: 8-12).

Their number is innumerable. In Daniel 7: 9-10 we read of God's throne: "a river of fire was flowing, coming out from before Him. Thousands upon thousands attended Him; ten thousand times ten thousand stood before Him." The Hebrew language had no word for *million* but instead used *a thousand thousands* for a million. *Ten thousand times ten thousand* would be a hundred million. The same words are used in Revelation 5:11: "Thousands upon thousands and ten thousand times ten thousand."

They were originally all holy. Angels were all created at the same time and are not born as humans are and do not marry and reproduce and multiply themselves. Angels are always spoken of in the masculine. They are always referred to as men, never as women. And when they appear in human form it is always as men, so there is no reproducing, or marriage among them.

The world of angels comes in two groupings: the good angels and the fallen angels and are organized into a hierarchy of different rankings with tremendous power and authority. The Bible speaks of "thrones," "Rulers and authority, powers and dominion" (Ephesians 1:21; Colossians 1:16). There has been continual warfare between the good and the fallen angels for the control of mankind throughout history.

The prince of darkness was there from the beginning of mankind and the history of the human race is a long scene of warfare and cruelty, pain and sorrow.

How terrible and fearful are the forces of darkness and spiritual wickedness that is behind all the sin and misery that has plagued fallen mankind throughout history. The believer in Christ has already won the victory. On the cross, Christ took upon Himself the judgment for the sins of the world and all the fury of the prince of darkness. Christ crushed Satan's head (Genesis 3:15) and He disarmed the satanic powers and authorities and triumphed over them by the cross (Colossians 2:13-15). And every believer shares in His triumph. As David was Israel's champion when he defeated Goliath (I Samuel 17:45-51) and the Israelites shared in his victory (I Samuel 17:52-54), Christ is the believer's Champion and we share in His victory (Ephesians 2:4-7).

The ministry of angels is important to the understanding of God's providential care and leading of His people. Believers are surrounded by holy angels, mighty beings sent from God to minister to His children (Hebrews 1:14) throughout their lifetimes, and to carry them home to heaven when their journey here is over (Luke 16:22).

They were present all through the history of the human race. They were at the beginning of creation: "Where were you when I laid the earth's foundation? Tell me if you understand. Who marked off its dimensions? Surely you know! Who stretched a measuring line across it? On what were its footings set, or who laid its cornerstone – while the morning stars sang together and all the angels shouted for joy?" (Job 38:4-7).

The world makes jokes about the devil and relegates him to the realm of myth. He is commonly pictured as wearing a red costume and having horns and a tail and carrying a pitchfork. However, a correct knowledge of this malignant being is vital to any real understanding of the history of the world we live in and the personal conflict in which we are involved.

The existence, power and schemes of the devil are facts of tremendous significance, for we live in the midst of his schemes and snares. Jesus informs us that Satan heads a mighty kingdom of fallen angels called demons.

He is the malignant spirit who first tempted mankind to sin through our first parents, Adam and Eve. Since then his purpose has been to drive a wedge between mankind and their Creator. His goal is to hurt God the only way he can and that is through mankind whom God loves. His goal is nothing short of the eternal ruin of mankind.

In the process of his war with God, he has brought untold sorrow and shame to the history of the human race. He is the instigator of wars and hatred between mankind.

The world is deceived by this great deceiver, whom Jesus called the father of lies, to the point of rendering him a mere fable. This greatly enhances his influence and advantage over men, for your greatest enemy is the one you do not know you have. He is the motivating influence behind the world's mindset against the things of God.

Because mankind is born under his influence, they are unaware of it. He is the motivating spirit behind the present world-system at war with God. The Bible gives a detailed description of this person and his career. It describes a being so powerful and influential that all would be lost apart from the One who came to "destroy the works of the devil" (I John 3:8).

CHAPTER 1
LUCIFER'S CREATION AND FALL

Ezekiel 38:11-19 and Isaiah 14:12-15 deal with Satan's creation and fall. He was created a glorious Cherub named *Lucifer* meaning "Morning Star" (Isaiah 14:12). He was the most exalted of the angelic beings, but through his pride, he became Satan the Devil. In Isaiah 14, God speaks beyond the king of Babylon (Isaiah 13:1) and in Ezekiel 28 beyond the king of Tyre (Ezekiel 28:1) to the motivating influence behind them. An example of this is seen in Matthew 16:23, where Jesus spoke beyond Peter, who was rebuking Jesus for saying that He must be crucified, to address Satan who was the motivating influence behind what Peter said.

In Ezekiel 28:13, he is said to have been in the Garden of Eden. Certainly, this could not be true of the ruler of Tyre. But Satan the Tempter was there.

Ezekiel 28:14 says he was ordained by God to be a "guardian Cherub," and that he was on the holy mount of God: "you walked among the fiery stones." Lucifer was the greatly exalted Cherub who guarded or covered God's throne with praises as he led the other angels in the worship of God.

The mountain of God was a symbol of God's throne and center of government. The "fiery stones" refer to angels. "You were blameless in all your ways till wickedness was found in you" (Ezekiel 28:15). Many wonder why God would create the devil and evil, but the truth is that God created Lucifer and all the angels with free wills, in the same way He created mankind. God created mankind and the angels with a choice to love Him or rebel against Him.

If He created them as mere robots they could not truly love their Creator.

His exalted position and close proximity to God's throne caused him to covet God's glory and worship. "Your heart became proud on account of your beauty, and you corrupted your wisdom because of your splendor" (Ezekiel 28:17).

Isaiah 14:12-15 tells of his fall from his lofty position: "How have you fallen from heaven, O morning star, son of the dawn! You have been cast down to the earth, you who once laid low the nations! You said in your heart, 'I will ascend to heaven; I will raise my throne above the stars of God; I will sit enthroned on the mount of assembly, on the utmost height of the sacred mountain. I will ascend above the tops of the clouds; I will make myself like the Most High.' But you are brought down to the grave, to the depths of the pit."

The prophet Isaiah announces the fall of this mighty angel and the reason for it and some of its results – "you laid low the nations." Much of this is yet future and prophetic of his terrible impact upon the earth.

Lucifer the anointed Cherub became Satan the devil and was cast out of his position in the third heaven to the lower heavenly places (the second heaven – Ephesians 6:12) and became "the ruler of the kingdom of the air, the spirit who is now at work in those who are disobedient" (Ephesians 2:2). He now stands as prince of the organized kingdom of darkness opposed to the kingdom of light. This will be his realm until the time of the end when Michael the archangel will cast him and his angels to the earth during the tribulation period (Revelation 12:7-13).

His great ambition was to have a throne of his own and be worshipped by mankind and to rule over the "stars of heaven" – the angels. Much of this has already been allowed by God, with Satan's recognized authority in the heavenly and earthly realms. It will reach its climax during the great tribulation under the antichrist's reign.

CHAPTER 2
MANKIND'S CREATION AND FALL

God's purpose in creating mankind was so He could communicate Himself with His creation in a love relationship to present a bride to Christ. Because God is love, He created mankind as a spiritual personality on whom He could bestow His love. His desire was to pour out His love and glory to fill His creation and have it reveal His beauty and majesty.

He created mankind for a relationship with Himself. This is the purpose for which mankind was created in God's image. He had to create them in His own image, so they could return His love, just as Eve was created in Adam's image to be his companion (Genesis 2:21-22). We are told in Hebrews 2:5-6 that God created mankind in order to make him ruler over the angels and the world to come. They would rule under his authority as the bride of Christ: "It is not to angels that he has subjected the world to come, about which we are speaking. But there is a place where someone has testified: "what is man that you are mindful of him, the son of man that you care for him. You made him a little lower than the angels; you crowned him with glory and honor and put everything under his feet."

The Bible is filled with promises of a glorious eternal destiny that God has provided for redeemed mankind: "No eye has seen, no ear has heard, no mind has conceived what God has prepared for those who love Him" (Hebrews 2:9). The Bible teaches a most exalted purpose for man's creation. This purpose is to have perfect fellowship with God Himself and to share in His eternal life and His ruling of the universe in a family relationship. This is why mankind was created in God's image.

Hebrews 2:11 tells us: "Both the one who makes men holy (God) and those who are made holy (believers) are of the same family. So Jesus is not ashamed to call them brothers." And we read in Matthew 12:48-50: "Jesus replied to them, 'who is my mother, and who are my brothers?' Pointing to his disciples, He said, 'Here are my mother and my brothers. For whoever does the will of My Father in heaven is my brother and sister and mother."

In John 17: 20-24, we read, "My prayer is not for them alone. I pray also for those who will believe in me through their message, that all of them may be one, Father, just as you are in me and I am in you. May they also be in us so that the world may believe that you have sent Me. I have given them the glory that you gave me. May they be brought to complete unity to let the world know that you sent me and have loved them even as you have loved me. Father I want those you have given me to be with me where I am, and to see my glory, the glory you have given me because you loved me before the creation of the world."

God has an eternal plan for each believer's life. He wanted to reveal Himself in His triune essence, which is an eternal, loving relationship. He created them with free will so they could return His love willingly, not as mere programmed robots. Love must be given willingly and freely.

Because God is All-knowing, He knew mankind would sin and fall, so He built into His plan of creation His plan of redemption. Jesus Christ, a member of the Triune God was appointed to be "the Lamb slain before the foundation of the world" (Revelation 3:8). The One slain before the foundation of the world was "Before all things, and in Him all things hold together. And He is the head of the body, the church" (Colossians 1: 17-18a).

"He was before all things." He was before history itself, in fact He is the starting point of history: "In the beginning was the Word, and the Word was with God. He was with God in the beginning. Through Him all things were made; without Him nothing was made that has been made" (John 1:3). And the history that began in Him is controlled and directed by Him. As the Logos, He upholds or sustains creation by the "mighty power of His command," with a single specific purpose in view.

The universe, especially planet earth, was created for one purpose: to provide a suitable home for the redeemed and glorified human race. They were created in the image and likeness of God for the one purpose of providing an eternal companion for the Son. The Messiah came with the one intent: to give birth to the church and to obtain His companion in the figure of a bride. Thus, the church does not refer merely to everyone who is a member of a church or who simply claims to be a *Christian*, but to those who have been truly "born again."

Jesus declared, "I tell you the truth, no one can see the kingdom of God unless he is born again" (John 1:3). The church is the *called out* body of redeemed mankind. All members of this church have been called out of the world (cosmos) under judgment, into a new sphere of existence, as a new creation through faith in Christ. All things belong to the church and are for her benefit: "All things are yours, whether Paul or Apollos or Cephas or the world or life or death or the present or the future – all are yours, and you are of Christ, and Christ is of God" (I Corinthians 3:22-23). Not only does He sustain and uphold his creation, He is moving it toward a specific goal according to His eternal plan.

This was the revelation of the truth revealed to Paul when he wrote: "And we know that in all things God works for the good of those who love Him (the church), who have been called according to His purpose (as His Bride)" (Romans 8:28). God's purpose for creation was that His Son should have an eternal companion described in Revelation 21:9 as "The bride, the wife of the Lamb," one to whom God will give His heart and share His rule.

The Biblical teaching is that Christ died for all men, but in a limited sense. Christ's death and resurrection did PROVIDE redemption for ALL mankind. No one was left out: "He is the atoning sacrifice for our sins, and not only for ours but also for the sins of the whole world" (I John 2:2). All who have ever been born since the dawn of human history are included in God's redeeming Love.

Christ died for all men but in a limited sense as we are told in John 1:9-13: "The true light that gives light to every man was coming into the world. He was in the world, and though the world was made through Him, the world did not recognize Him. He came to that which was His own, but His own did not receive Him (referring to the Jews as a nation). Yet to all who did receive Him (individual Jews and gentiles), to those who believed in His name, He gave the right to become the children of God – children born not of natural descent, nor of human decision or a husbands will, but born of God."

So we see that while Christ died for all men, only those who receive Him by faith actually enter into the benefits of His death and resurrection. The intimate relationship that God wants with mankind cannot be forced upon them but must be freely chosen. God knew from all eternity that the result of His creation and redemptive work would only be for a tiny minority comparatively speaking who would benefit. Thus it was to possess this small group, called the *Church* (Matthew 16:18) and "the Bride, the lamb's wife" (Revelation 21:9), that God created the universe, and entered into human history and suffered and died.

"For He chose us in Him before the creation of the world to be holy and blameless in His sight" (Ephesians 1:4). In eternity past, God had certain purposes or goals to be accomplished. Those who are *in Christ* would be holy and blameless in His sight. God's purpose of creation is that those *in Him* – in Christ – would be a holy people. For that purpose, God created Adam and Eve, and knowing that mankind would sin and fall, God determined to carry out His purpose in Christ. This purpose will be fulfilled when Christ returns for His bride who will be presented to Him "without fault and with great joy" (Jude 24).

God purposed in His heart to bring about creation, for whom Christ would suffer and die, in order to bring about a holy people who would be the Father's love gift to His Son. As believers in Christ, we will be in the world for only a little while. Though we are in the world, we are not of the world, but belong to Christ, purchased by His blood, and chosen before the foundation of this world. We were made for another world. We do not belong to this world but are merely passing through it to another.

Much of the Bible is history written in advance. If we want to know the purpose of history we must read the last chapter of the Bible, the Book of Revelation. In it we find the goal of history. It is Christ's eternal companion, His spotless bride, united with Him forever at the "wedding of the Lamb" (Revelation 21:8).

The background of this is presented in John 14:2-3 in the form of an oriental marriage. "In my Father's house are many rooms; if it were not so, I would have told you. I am going there to prepare a place for you. And if I go and prepare a place for you, I will come back and take you to be with me that you also may be where I am."

In the oriental marriage, after the engagement and the dowry was paid, the bridegroom would go to his father's house and prepare rooms there for His future bride. When this was completed, the bridegroom would return for His bride and take her to his father's house to be united in marriage. The time of the bridegroom's return was unknown to the bride. In the same manner, Christ's return will take place at the rapture of the Church when the bride will be glorified and made perfectly holy. As the bridegroom's return was unknown to the bride, the time of the rapture is unknown to the church today.

The blood-bought and blood-washed Church is the goal of history. This was foreshadowed in the wedding of Adam and Eve in Genesis Chapter 2, when God took a rib out of the side of Adam and created Eve in Adam's image and brought her to Adam as his wife. It was always God's plan that out of Christ's pierced side He would form the church and present her to Him as His companion in the figure of a bride.

According to Ephesians 5:25, we see that human marriage is a foreshadow of the relationship between Christ and the church: "Husbands, love your wives, just as Christ loved the church and gave Himself up for her." This refers to Christ's sacrifice on the cross, which was the dowry price paid to seal the engagement or betrothal. The church is engaged to Christ.

At the time that this was written, engagement was considered sacred, just as though the couple were married, although they still lived with their parents. Paul refers to this in II Corinthians 11:2: "I am jealous for you with a godly jealousy. I promised you to one husband, to Christ, so that I might present you as a pure virgin to Him." The future bride was to stay pure for her future husband while waiting for him to come for her and receive her in marriage.

As the body of Christ the church is inseparable from the Head.

As the bride of Christ she will sit enthroned with Him as His queen. "To him who overcomes, I will give the right to sit WITH ME ON MY THRONE, just as I overcame and sat down on My Father's throne. He who has an ear let him hear what the Spirit says to the churches" (Revelation 3:21). The King and His queen will both sit side by side on the same throne of the universe. Then God's eternal plan for the ages will begin to unfold.

Until then, the entire creation is under the Son's control and is being regulated by Him, as we are told in Hebrews 1:3: "The Son is the radiance of God's glory and the exact representation of His being, sustaining all things by His powerful Word."

So here we see that the Son is sustaining or upholding all things. This also includes the thought of moving all things toward a specific goal, when He will dwell with His people. All history finds its meaning in Christ.

The angels were created before mankind was created (Job 38:7). Their purpose was to "serve those who will inherit salvation" (Hebrews 1:14). Lucifer's fall occurred shortly before mankind's creation. He renounced his allegiance to the Most High and became the leader of an unnumbered host of fallen angels called demons, referred to as the rulers of this present age of darkness, the spiritual hosts of wickedness in the heavenly realms, an organized hierarchy of fallen angels.

He became the great adversary of God and accuser and slanderer of His people. From that time on, there has been a great division in the cosmos, as an opposing kingdom of darkness was born to challenge the universal kingdom of God. God allowed this to happen for His own purposes. He would allow the devil to have his way within the limits of God's overruling will. He allows these things to take place for our good that we may love Him of our own free will and choose Him as our Savior from the darkness of sin.

This is why we are told in 1 Peter 4:12, "Do not be surprised at the painful trial you are suffering, as though something strange were happening to you." And the Lord Jesus tells us why it will work for our good. "In this world you will have trouble. But take heart! I have overcome the world" (John 16:33). It would allow God to reveal the depth of His love for His fallen creation and allow mankind freedom to choose Him or reject Him. God created mankind for a mutually chosen relationship.

Through the church, God will reveal Himself to the holy angels, as we are told in Ephesians 3:10-11: "His intent was that now, through the church, the manifold wisdom of God should be made known to the rulers and authorities in the heavenly realms, according to His eternal purpose which He accomplished in Christ Jesus our Lord." And "In order that in the coming ages He might show the incomparable riches of His grace expressed in His kindness to us in Christ Jesus" (Ephesians 2:7).

The Lord is using the church, the result of His cosmic victory at the cross, to reveal to the angels, both fallen and holy, the greatness of God's love and wisdom in His redemption of mankind. We are being watched by the angelic hosts who were "sent to serve those who will inherit salvation" (Hebrews 1:14). Every time a lonely missionary wins a soul to Christ, seeming unknown by anyone, God leads the angels in rejoicing before His throne (Luke 15: 7 and 10).

The very ones who were once the captives of Satan are now on display as God's eternal trophy to His love and grace, and are now "To the praise of His glorious grace" (Ephesians 1:6). And they proclaim the Gospel of the demise of Satan's kingdom. The whole cosmos is in bondage to sin and its effects, and salvation is a cosmic event affecting the whole creation as well as believers. It is the redemption of the whole world process.

The angels, who were filled with awe and praise for His power and wisdom in creation, would now be filled with praise for the riches of His grace revealed in His redemption of sinners. A new inexhaustible source of praise is being manifested in God's marvelous work of redemption.

God formed man on the sixth day of creation: "The Lord God formed the man of the dust of the ground and breathed into his nostrils the breath of life, and the man became a living being" (Genesis 2:7).

The basic chemical elements of the earth were used to make man's physical body. God then energized the man's body with the breath of life. Here we have a very intimate picture of God forming man's body and then kneeling down and breathing directly into him.

"Now the Lord God planted a garden in the east, in Eden, and there He had put the man He had formed, and the Lord God made all kinds of trees to grow out of the ground – trees that were pleasing to the eye and good for food. In the middle of the garden was the tree of the knowledge of good and evil" (Genesis 2: 8-9).

Mankind was created for fellowship with God; and knowing that man would fall, God planned, through Christ, to demonstrate the incomparable riches of His grace expressed in His kindness to us in Christ Jesus" (Ephesians 2:7). God prepares a special area, a perfect garden with beautiful trees bearing delicious fruit of every kind, for his home. It was called *Eden* which means *delight*; it was paradise.

Adam was the representative of all his descendants and would set the course for humanity and human history. In the center of the garden were the tree of life and the tree of the knowledge of good and evil – so called because evil would be known if man disobeyed God and good if man obeyed Him.

"And the Lord God commanded the man, 'you are free to eat from any tree in the garden; but you must not eat from the tree of the knowledge of good and evil, for when you eat of it you will surely die'" (Genesis 2:15-17). Then Eve was created. "But for Adam no suitable helper was found. So the Lord God caused the man to fall into a deep sleep; and while he was sleeping, He took one of the man's ribs and closed up the place with flesh. Then the Lord God made a woman from the rib He had taken out of the man, and He brought her to the man" (Genesis 2:20-22). This represented the giving away of the bride to the groom in marriage.

CHAPTER 3
MANKIND'S FALL
AND THE PROMISED REDEEMER

Satan knew that the only way he could hurt God was through mankind so that was his point of attack. In his consuming hatred of God, Satan would wage war against the human race that God loved. The devil and his demonic hoards were about to begin the conflict of the ages. God, who could have ended the conflict before it began, would allow it to play itself out for good.

He would use it to reveal Himself to His creation through His dealings with sin and its terrible consequences for the sinner and reveal His love and grace to His creation as nothing else could. The drama of angelic and human rebellion and His response to it would reveal to His creation the character of their God.

"Now the serpent was more crafty than any of the wild animals the Lord God had made. The devil had taken over the body of the serpent. He said to the woman: "Did God really say, you must not eat of any tree in the garden?" (Genesis 3:1). Satan asked this question as though he had overheard this and could not believe what he heard. He distorts what God said. God had actually told Adam that he was free to eat from every tree but one.

"The woman said to the serpent, 'We may eat fruit from the trees in the garden, but God did say 'You must not eat fruit from the tree that is in the middle of the garden, and you must not touch it, or you will die'" (Genesis 3: 2-4).

It has also been pointed out that Eve also misquoted what God had said when she added, "And you must not touch it." But I rather think that Adam told her this as an added precaution. God had instructed Adam, and Adam would have passed this instruction on to Eve. " Don't eat of the tree that is in the middle of the garden," and I suspect Adam added, "in fact don't even touch it!"

The serpent's body was taken over by Lucifer, who had earlier led the angels in a revolt against God. He would now tempt God's human creation. Jesus would later, during His earthly ministry, refer to this event when He said the devil was "a murderer and a liar from the beginning" (John 8:44). He snuck into the garden like a thief and Jesus said, "The thief comes only to steal, kill and destroy" (John 10:10).

"You shall not surely die," the serpent said to the woman. "For God knows that when you eat of it your eyes will be opened and you will be like God, knowing good and evil" (Genesis 3: 4-5).

If Satan can get us to question God's word or His goodness, we fall into his trap. The woman saw what the tempter wanted her to see. Then her own lusts took over and each step became easier until she took and ate. At this point, they had taken control of their own lives. They had made themselves their own masters, which is the very essence of sin. Now instead of God, they would write the unwritten history of the human race. Their own individual wills had replaced the will of God.

"Then the eyes of both of them were opened, and they realized they were naked; so they sewed fig-leaves together and made coverings for themselves." Then they heard the sound of the Lord God as He was walking in the garden. It was a Theophany of the Word of God, The pre-incarnate Christ, and they hid from Him among the trees of the garden, but the Lord God called out to Adam and said to him, "Where are you?" He answered, "I heard you in the garden, and I was afraid because I was naked; so I hid myself" (Genesis 3:8-10).

Through sin Satan had driven a wedge between God and humanity. Though Adam was covered with fig leaves, he knew that he was still naked before God. God was seeking confession and repentance but instead Adam blamed Eve and Eve blamed the serpent (Genesis 3:11-13).

"So the Lord God said to the serpent, 'because you have done this, cursed are you above all the livestock and all the wild animals! You will crawl on your belly and you will eat dust all the days of your life. And I will put enmity between you and the woman, and between your offspring and hers; He will crush your head, and you will strike His heel'" (Genesis 3: 14-15).

To the woman God announced that she would give birth with increased pain and there would be strife between the man and the woman. From now on they would enter the world under the curse. Birth would be a time of struggle and pain as a constant reminder that we are all sinners (Genesis 3:16).

Adam was told that the ground would be cursed. Now only through pain and toil would it produce fruit, along with weeds and thorns. Their bodies would begin to age and wear out and finally die and return to the dust of the ground from which they came.

As a result of their sin, the serpent would be cursed above all the other animals. The serpent was to be a perpetual reminder to mankind of their fall and Satan's final doom. It may have stood erect and glided on its tail, but now it would crawl in the dust as an object of revulsion.

In the heavenly realm, Lucifer's sin had brought about a fall among the angels prior to the fall of Adam and Eve. The fallen angels are also called demons. There is only one Devil, which means *Slanderer* or *Accuser*. He is called *Satan* which means *Resister*. He is the chief of the fallen angels who tempted mankind to fall.

Angels fell individually, but humans fell corporately. *In Adam*, we all fell. Because Adam was the head or organic representative, death established itself on all of his descendants as well. Through Adam, every member of the human race, through his or her mere birth, is inescapably a member of a fallen and corrupted race.

This is why Jesus declared, "I tell you the truth. No one can see the kingdom of God unless he is born again" (John 3:3).

Satan became the "prince of this world" (John 12:31; 14:30), and the "god of this age" [mindset] (II Corinthians 4:4). The whole world is under his control (I John 5:19), and he is the "spirit working in the children of disobedience" (Ephesians 2: 2). He is the Tempter (Matthew 4:3). He is a "liar and the father of lies" (John 8:44), the deceiver who leads the whole world astray (Revelation 12:9).

Then, in the midst of sin and its horror and shame, God gave a promise that He would not allow the enemy to destroy His intended purpose for His creation of an intimate relationship with Himself. It was the beginning of the gospel message, the message of the Offspring of the woman, born of a virgin, not connected to the fallen nature of its parents. Not tainted by the fall and not under sin's dominion. The term "offspring of the woman" is unique because generation was through the male.

The only remedy now was a new creation brought about by a new Head of humanity, another Adam, the Last Adam, to undo the tragedy caused by the first Adam. This was God's plan from the beginning. God would send His own Son as the Last Adam to undo the works of the Devil. Out of the ruins of the old creation *in Adam*, God would build His new creation *in Christ*. "For as in Adam all die, so in Christ all will be made alive" (I Corinthians 15:22).

In Eden God decreed enmity, meaning bitter hatred, between the serpent's offspring and the Offspring of the woman. The primary offspring of the woman (A virgin birth) was the Lord Jesus Christ. The primary offspring of the serpent is Satan.

Since this first Messianic prophecy was given, Satan has been the bitter enemy of the woman's Seed, The Lord Jesus Christ. His Person and work have been the focus of Satan's attack.

The secondary seed are the *children of the kingdom* and the *children of the wicked one*. This enmity of Satan is also directed toward God's people. He makes unceasing war on believers to mar their life and service because they are "partakers of the divine nature" (II Peter 1:4), and to them has been committed the task of carrying on Christ's work, the great ministry of reconciliation, that through them, their witness and prayers, the truths of salvation through Christ will be given out.

And because of this, we can expect the fiercest opposition from Satan. This is why Jesus prayed, "My prayer is not that you take them out of the world but that you protect them from the evil one" (John 17: 15). Satan's attack on our effective witness will be noticeable especially in our prayer life which will literally become a war zone.

The children of the kingdom are those who trust in Christ. "For you are all the children of God through faith in Christ Jesus" (Galatians 3:26). The children of the serpent are those who reject Christ – "You brood of snakes" (Matthew 12: 34). "Snakes! Sons of vipers! How will you escape the judgment of hell?" (Matthew 23:33). "For you are children of your father the Devil" (John 8:44).

In this struggle, the offspring of the woman would crush Satan's head with a fatal deathblow and destroy the works of the devil: "the Son of Man came to destroy the works of the devil" (I John 3:8). But in the process of crushing the serpent's head, He would have to expose His heel to the serpent's deadly fangs. This would take place on the cross where Christ would destroy the works of Satan for those who would trust in Him, but to do this would cost the Son of God great suffering and death to redeem us from the penalty of sin. But He would rise again triumphantly after crushing Satan's head.

This cosmic warfare between good and evil would be the theme of human history and the unfolding story revealed in the Scriptures. From then on, Satan would be on alert for signs of the arrival of the coming Redeemer to prevent His coming to crush his head. Christ's coming signaled the greatest explosion of activity from the demonic realm, and His coming would eventually seal their doom. God has a plan for this world. It will be the scene of Divine visitation. It will be the scene of the cosmic war where God will defeat the Evil one.

In the fullness of God's time Jesus Christ, the eternal Son of God, became flesh as the offspring of the virgin. He was conceived by the Holy Spirit, but born of the virgin Mary. He was born of Mary, but the One who was born already existed from eternity. He would come as the Second Adam, the Captain of our salvation, ever moving forward on the lonely road toward suffering and death to crush the serpents head and "destroy the devil's work" (1 John 3:8).

Adam and Eve experienced spiritual death, which is separation from God; and physical death began in their bodies, and this would be passed on to their descendants. Sin and death are inherited from birth: "Therefore, just as sin entered the world through one man, and death through sin, and in this way death came to all men, because all sinned" (Romans 5:12) and a curse was put upon the earth because of their sin: "For the creation was subjected to frustration"(Romans 8:20).

Adam was created in the image of God, but now that image was marred and barely recognizable, and now the malignant result would be passed on to the whole human race. Later, Adam would have a son in his own image. Their first son, Cain, became the first murderer (Genesis 4:8), a clear reminder that something was very wrong with the creation that God had declared *very good*.

The pleasant life of Eden, characterized by fellowship with God, came to a sudden end. Mankind was created to have dominion over God's creation, but their choice to heed the voice of the Tempter and disobey God changed everything. His dominion over the earth was lost to the Tempter, and the devil became the "prince of this world" (John 14:30), and I John 5:19 tells us ". . . the whole world lies under the control of the evil one." Jesus referred to Satan as the "prince of this world" (John 12:31; John 14:30; and John 16:11).

This is brought out in Luke 4:5-8 during Jesus confrontation with the devil: "The devil led Him up to a high place and showed Him in an instant all the kingdoms of the world. And he said to him, 'I will give you all their authority and splendor, for it has been given to me, and I can give it to anyone I want to. So if you worship me, it will all be yours.'"

It is significant that Jesus did not dispute Satan's claim to own the kingdoms of this world. Jesus came to go to the cross to reclaim from Satan what Adam had forfeited. Satan was saying that Jesus did not have to go to the cross. He could have these kingdoms if He would bow down and worship him.

But Jesus rebuked his offer. He chose rather to die for the sin of the world and establish His own kingdom.

Thus when Satan claimed that he could give all the authority and splendor of all the kingdoms of the world, for they belonged to him, Jesus did not dispute him.

Eventually the antichrist will take him up on this offer (Revelation 13: 1-2).

Adam and Eve were driven out of the garden. The perfect creation that God had declared "very good" (Genesis 1:31), was now devastated by the fall of angels in the heavenly realm who had set themselves up against the Creator. This was soon followed by the sin of mankind in the earthly realm. This has resulted in the deadly conflict between good and evil since the dawn of human history. The tragedy is that the vast majority of mankind is unaware of this warfare in which the enemy wants nothing short of the eternal damnation of the human race.

From that day until now, the history of mankind has been one of warfare between the spiritual powers of good and evil, between the Creator and the created. Mankind is the focal point of the satanic schemes and ambitions because the only way Satan could hurt God was through mankind. God's reaction to our sin and suffering would dumbfound the wildest imagination. It would show the extent to which He would go to redeem His fallen creation.

As a consequence of this, the Church is now engaged in a spiritual warfare with the spiritual forces of Satan's kingdom. Now, all the hatred of Satan against God is directed toward the church. All the power of his demonic forces is now activated to rob the finished work of Christ of its full effect upon the world. His warfare with the Head of the church is directed against the members of His spiritual body. The devil is a shrewd general and uses his troops where most needed and that is why his target is Bible-believing churches and believers. We are commissioned by the Lord to carry on His work, and this makes us very dangerous to Satan's cause. He sows the weeds among the wheat, the false among the true, the bad among the good. Deception and discourse are his method. This is why we are given so many warnings in the Bible not to be ignorant of Satan's devices and to stand on the finished work of Christ.

There are still battles to be fought. The victory over the powers of evil in principle has not yet been manifested. The Christian life is still spoken of in the New Testament in terms of warfare. The final outcome of this war has been settled, but there are still important battles to be fought and fighting these battles still defines the believer's life. When we finally enter into His presence, the glory and joy will render all the sufferings of this present world well worth it.

This is also why the Scriptures give us so many images of believers as soldiers. The believer's role in the world is one of conflict. Believers in every age are called upon to fight the good fight of faith. We are exhorted to walk in the footsteps of Jesus down the path of warfare and that means that this struggle between our Lord and Satan must be expressed through us. But many Christians have abandoned the battlefield and are unaware of the spiritual conflict.

Before He returns to set up His kingdom, it is God's plan that the gospel be preached to the ends of the earth. And while His people are carrying out the great commission, the warfare will continue as Satan resists our every move to proclaim the gospel. He will continue to blind unbelievers to the gospel.

This conflict of the ages is referred to by Jesus in Matthew 13: 37-43: "The one who sowed the good seed is the Son of Man. The field is the world, and the good seed stands for the sons of the kingdom. The weeds are the sons of the evil one, and the enemy who sows them is the devil. The harvest is at the end of the age, and the harvesters are angels.

"As the weeds are pulled up and burned in the fire, so it will be at the end of the age. The Son of Man will send out

His angels, and they will weed out of His kingdom everything that causes sin and all who do evil. They will throw them into the fiery furnace, where there will be weeping and gnashing of teeth. Then the righteous will shine like the sun in the kingdom of their Father. He who has ears let Him hear" (Matthew 13:40-43).

"Do not be like Cain, who belonged to the evil one and murdered his brother. And why did he murder him? Because his own actions were evil and his brother's were righteous" (I John 3:12).

CHAPTER 4
SATAN'S DEFEAT AT THE CROSS

Genesis 3:15 heralds that Messiah will ultimately end the age-long conflict with Satan by crushing his head.

Jesus said "But if I drive out demons by the Spirit of God, then the kingdom of God has come upon you. Or again, how can anyone enter a strong man's house and carry off his possessions unless he first ties up the strong man? Then he can rob his house" (Matthew 12: 28-29).

Jesus is saying that one cannot take back the property of Satan's kingdom unless he first ties up the fully armed strong man who is in charge of the whole operation. This is what Jesus came to do. The account of Jesus' ministry begins with Jesus confronting the devil in the desert. His ministry was about overcoming the *strong man* – Satan – who was guarding his property, and enabling His people to take his possessions (his captives who have been blinded to the gospel).

Before going to the cross, the battle was joined in Gethsemane. Satan's legions put intense pressure on Jesus as He contemplated the cross. His will was attacked at every point. "His sweat was like drops of blood falling to the ground," as He considered what lay ahead of Him.

Here we learn that soldiers of the cross win the battle in the spiritual realm of prayer. We win our most crucial battles by insisting "Thy will be done," whatever the cost to one's self. There are times when we must enter into the wrestling of the self-dependent Jacob when God contends with us in order to break our will of self-sufficiency that is so common in all of us. It is through this struggle that He transforms us into His God-dependent Israel.

At the cross, the cosmic war that has raged from the beginning had now come to center on one person. The One stronger than *the strong man* had finally arrived. After defeating Satan in His own life, the Son of Man was qualified to defeat him for the entire cosmos.

Unlike the rest of humanity, Jesus did not come under Satan's power, as He said in John 14:30-31, "I will not speak with you much longer, for the prince of this world is coming. He has no hold on me. But the world must learn that I love the Father and that I do exactly what My Father has commanded me." Satan had no hold on Him and, as the Last Adam He would go to the cross and crush the serpent's head as His Father had commanded Him.

On the cross, Jesus struck the fatal blow to Satan's kingdom. After His resurrection and glorification, He is now seated as our representative at the right hand of God the Father. Christ is now the true prince of the world and will return to establish His kingdom. Satan's claim to this world is as a usurper. Nothing Satan can do can change the finality of his defeat at the cross.

In John 12:31-33, Jesus said, "Now is the time for judgment on this world, now the prince of this world will be driven out. But I, when I am lifted up from the earth, will draw all men to myself. He said this to show the kind of death He was going to die." The phrase *driven out* is even stronger in the Greek: *driven completely out*. It is a total defeat at the cross. Satan will continue to resist throughout this age, but the outcome has already been settled in the death and resurrection of Jesus.

Through the death and resurrection of Jesus, Satan would be driven out (John 12:31). A new *strong man* and rightful ruler has been enthroned. Ephesians 1:18-23 speaks of the cosmic dimension of Christ's resurrection: "I pray also that the eyes of your heart may be enlightened in order that you may know the hope to which He has called you, the riches of His glorious inheritance in the saints, and His incomparably great power for us who believe. That power is like the working of His mighty strength, which He exerted in Christ when He raised Him from the dead and seated Him at His right hand in the heavenly realms, far above all rule and authority, power and dominion, and every title that can be given, not only in the present age but also in the one to come. And God placed all things under His feet and appointed Him to be head over everything for the church, which is His body, the fullness of Him who fills everything in every way."

In Ephesians 2:1-7, Paul shows how all this applies to the position of believers. He shows how we were once part of the condemned world under the power of Satan and under God's wrath. But through His victory in His death and resurrection, Christ has overthrown Satan's kingdom by purchasing us out of the slave market of sin. We are no longer under Satan's authority, but share in Christ's victory over sin, death and hell. We have been raised far above it, and now we share in all the inheritance that belongs to Christ. Our position and standing has been fundamentally changed and we are a *new creation* (II Corinthians 5:17):

"As for you, you were dead in your transgressions and sins, in which you used to live when you followed the ways of this world and of the ruler of the kingdom of the air, the spirit who is now at work in those who are disobedient. All of us also lived among them at one time, gratifying the cravings of our sinful nature and following its sinful desires and thoughts. Like the rest, we were by nature objects of wrath. But because of His great love for us, God, who is rich in mercy, made us alive with Christ even when we were dead in transgressions. It is by grace you have been saved. And God raised us up in Christ and seated us with Him in the heavenly realms in Christ Jesus, in order that in the coming ages He might show the incomparable riches of His grace, expressed in His kindness to us in Christ Jesus" (Ephesians 2:1-7).

Colossians 2:14-15 says, "Having cancelled the written code, with its regulations that was against us and that stood opposed to us; He took it away, nailing it to the cross. And having disarmed the powers and authorities, He made a public spectacle of them, triumphing over them by the cross."

By dying for our sins and satisfying the law that demands death, Christ disarmed or stripped away the weapons of the satanic powers. This refers to the power of these demonic rulers to condemn believers through the broken law. They have been stripped of their power over believers who stand perfectly righteous and holy in Jesus Christ.

"Having cancelled the written code, with its regulations that was against us and that stood opposed to us" refers to the law that condemned us. God took away these broken laws by nailing them to Christ's cross and judging Him for them. The law (the written code) was a certificate of debt against us. In the east a debt was cancelled by nailing it to the post. Our certificate of guilt was taken out of the way by nailing it to the cross.

When Jesus was crucified, the Romans nailed the charges against Him to His cross, that He was claiming to be the king of the Jews (Matthew 27: 34-37). God nailed the record of our sins to His cross and judged Him for them and blotted them out: "Therefore, there is now no condemnation to those who are in Christ Jesus" (Romans 8:1). The certificate of our debt to the law has been cancelled because Christ paid our debt in full.

God became our blood relation through the incarnation – God taking on humanity through actual human birth bears the full penalty of the broken law in our behalf and pays the debt we owe but are unable to pay. He is our kinsman redeemer. It was customary that when the debt was paid the cancelled bill was nailed to a post for all to see. As with all debts, the only one who could sign its cancellation was the one to whom the debt was owed. The cross of Christ was God's signature on the cancelled debt written in Christ's blood.

Along with cancelling out the charges of the law against us, He also disarmed the evil spirit forces, Satan and his fallen angels, who ruled over us and were made a public spectacle by Christ's victory over them. Just as the victorious Romans would lead their defeated foes in a victory parade through the streets of Rome making a public spectacle of them.

Christ ascended to heaven after His resurrection as total victory over Satan and his demonic forces. When Christ sat down at the right hand of God, Satan's defeat was total, as He cried from the cross "it is finished" (John 19:30). Not only was the penalty for our sins paid for and finished, but Satan's legal authority and dominion was finished. But even more, when Jesus ascended to the throne of God, believers were raised and seated with Him: "But because of His great love for us, God who is rich in mercy, made us alive with Christ even when we were dead in transgressions; it is by grace you have been saved. And God raised us up in Christ and seated us with Him in the heavenly realms in Christ Jesus" (Ephesians 2:4-6).

In God's plan, the believer shares in the identity with Christ from the cross to the throne. According to Scripture, we were crucified with Him, buried with Him, raised with Him, exalted with Him, and seated on the throne with Him.

When Jesus defeated Satan, it was on our behalf. He did not need to conquer Satan for Himself. Satan had no authority over Him, as He said in John 14:30, "I will not speak with you much longer, for the prince of this world is coming. He has no hold on me." It was us that Satan had a hold on. The whole substitutionary work of Christ was in behalf of His bride. He took upon Himself humanity so He could take our place as our substitute and defeat Satan on our behalf.

Satan's dominion over us was ended at Calvary. This is the meaning of our enthronement with Christ. Now instead of Satan having authority over us, we have been given authority over him. Because believers are *in Christ* (Ephesians 1:1, 3, 9, 11, 13), the Father loves them as He loves Christ. In His prayer in John 17:23, Jesus prays for believers: "I in them and you in me. May they be brought to complete unity to let the world know that you sent Me. May they be brought to complete unity to let the world know that you sent me and have loved them even as you have loved me."

We are told in Revelation 5:1-10 that Christ holds the title deed to this world. Here we see a scroll with writing on both sides. This scroll contains God's will for the management of His creation. Scrolls have writing only on one side, but this has writing on both sides to show how full of blessing God's plan for His beloved creation is. This scroll has seven seals to keep his plan secure until the rightful heir opens it. God's purpose will be carried out only when each seal is broken. God's original plan was that mankind would rule the earth as God's representative. Heaven anxiously awaited the one who was worthy to take the scroll and break its seals, as a mighty angel called out in a loud voice for the rightful heir to come forward and John wept when no one came forward. All of Adam's descendants had forfeited the right to take the scroll (verses 2-4).

"Then one of the elders said to me, 'do not weep! See, the Lion of the tribe of Judah, the root of David has triumphed. He is able to open the scroll and its seven seals.'

Then I saw a Lamb, looking as if it had been slain, standing in the center of the throne, encircled by four living creatures and the elders. He had seven horns and seven eyes, which are the seven spirits of God sent out into all the earth. He came and took the scroll from the right hand of Him who sat upon the throne. And when He had taken it, the four living creatures and twenty-four elders fell down before the Lamb. Each one had a harp and they were holding golden bowls of incense which are the prayers of the saints. And they sang a new song: 'You are worthy to take the scroll and open its seals, because you were slain, and with your blood you purchased men for God from every tribe and language and people and nation. You have made them to be a kingdom and priests to serve our God, and they will reign on the earth'" (verses 5-10).

The "Lion of the Tribe of Judah" and the "Root of David" were Messianic terms for the heir of David's throne. One of the elders said to John that Messiah has prevailed to open the Book and break the seven seals (verse 6).

John looks around to see the Lion of Judah and in the midst of the throne he sees a lamb. The lamb John saw had been slain for sacrifice; but he was standing as resurrected. Horns were symbolic of power; seven horns would symbolize perfect or absolute power. Eyes were symbolic of knowledge and seven eyes represented perfect knowledge. The seven spirits of God refer to the seven-fold Holy Spirit (verse 6). When He had taken the scroll, the four beasts and twenty four elders fell down and worshipped before the Lamb. Each had a harp for singing praises to the Lamb and each had a golden bowl full of incense which are the prayers of the saints for the establishment of Christ's promised kingdom as Jesus taught us to pray: "Your kingdom come, your will be done on earth as it is in heaven" (Matt. 6:10).

They sang a new song of praise to the worthiness of the Lamb to take the scroll and open the seals and bring about the fulfillment of God's purpose because He died to redeem mankind for God and made them kings and priests, or literally a "kingdom of priests." Thus the fulfillment of God's purpose for mankind will be fulfilled by the Last Adam, the new Head of the redeemed humanity, Jesus Christ.

We are assured that Satan is a defeated foe. When Jesus disarmed Satan and his demons of their authority, He did it for us. Not only is Jesus their conqueror but so are those who are in Christ. Satan forever lost his authority over every one who belongs to Christ. They have been removed from his kingdom and are no longer of the world but have been transferred into the kingdom of Christ (Colossians 1:13; John 17: 6-26). But unbelievers are still of the world are part of Satan's kingdom. Satan is like a toothless lion. He can growl and intimidate, but he has no authority to back up his threats in the life of the believer.

CHAPTER 5
BORN TO BATTLE

In Matthew 16:16-19, Jesus uses Peter's confession to teach about the church. "Peter answered, 'You are the Christ, the Son of the living God.' Jesus replied 'Blessed are you, Simon son of Jonah, for this was not revealed to you by man, but by my Father in heaven. And I tell you that you are Peter, and on this rock I will build my church, and the gates of hades will not overcome it. I will give you the keys of the kingdom of heaven; whatever you bind on earth will be bound in heaven, and whatever you loose on earth will be loosed in heaven.'"

Here, the gates of hades are on the defensive, and God's church is on the offensive. Jesus says He is going to build His church on the Rock of Peter's confession that the Father had revealed to him – that Christ is the Son of the living God. Christ's church will be built by overcoming the gates of Satan's stronghold and releasing the prisoners he holds captive. They are to do this through the authority of Christ by the power of the gospel. The church is literally to storm the gates of hades in the power of the Holy Spirit. This is the reason Jesus established His church, which is His spiritual body in this dispensation of the Church. As Christ used His physical body at His first coming, He now uses His church.

The "keys of the kingdom of heaven" and "binding" and "loosing" has to do with the presentation of the gospel as does John 20:23: "If you forgive anyone his sins, they are forgiven; if you do not forgive them, they are not forgiven." If they believe, they are loosed from their sins; if they do not believe, they remain bound.

Only God can forgive sin, but the believer is given the authority of presenting the gospel message and declaring to those who believe that their sins are forgiven. It is the same with "binding" and "loosing." Those who believe the gospel are loosed from their sins; those who don't believe remain bound in their sins. This is to be the business of God's people. This is what the church is called to do.

Satan's great weapon is deception. He has an arsenal filled with lies – shrewd, subtle, convincing lies designed to mislead us. What we believe to be true, whether actually true or not, directly influences our choices in life. All of Satan's lies are for the one purpose: to prevent us from believing God and His Word. We must not allow him to intimidate us. He is the master of intimidation and seduction. The Bible informs us of his schemes so that he might not outwit us (II Corinthians 2:11).

The word *schemes* describes someone who is devious, sneaky, and unrelenting in his effort to destroy us. He outwits us by sinister and crafty strategies that he skillfully uses to outsmart us and set up a stronghold in our minds to control us. He uses discouragement that eventually leads to unbelief that we can win against him. This becomes a *stronghold* which must be torn down.

He infuses false thoughts about God into our minds – that God doesn't really care about us, that He would just as soon bless those who care nothing about Him while ignoring those who pray and struggle to serve Him. He sends thoughts that we might as well give up on Him, thereby destroying the foundation of our faith in a God who cares.

He is very artful in his deceptions to make things seem hopeless. His great desire is to break the ties of trust between the believer and God. This began in the Garden of Eden with his slander of God – that He is not trustworthy or truly worthy of our love. He sends his fiery arrows of doubt to cause us to lose heart.

The Bible not only informs us of the devil's schemes but also provides us with the weapon to defeat him. "The weapons we fight with are not the weapons of the world. On the contrary, they have divine power to demolish strongholds. We demolish arguments and every pretension that sets itself up against the knowledge of God and we take captive every thought to make it obedient to Christ" (2 Corinthians 10:4-5). God's answer to discouragement is the Word of God that informs us that we can do "Everything through Him who gives me strength" (Philippians 4:13).

Hebrews 12:1-3 gives us the key to victory over discouragement and losing heart in the battle: "Let us fix our eyes on Jesus, the Author and Perfecter of our faith, who for the joy set before Him endured the cross, scorning the shame, and sat down at the right hand of the throne of God. Consider Him who endured such opposition from sinful men, so that you will not grow weary and lose heart."

Hebrews 11 gives a summary of past heroes of the faith who are held up as examples to encourage us to run the race of this life. In a race, the runner is to discard everything that hinders his running. They are to strip down of every weight that would hinder them, especially the sin that so easily entangles our feet in carrying out the will of God. [The context of chapter 11 shows this sin to be unbelief.] We are to persevere under pressure or stress, determined to finish our race with honor. We are to endure trials with a faith that perseveres and will not give up.

It is our trust in the Lord that causes us to persevere in His strength. We are to keep our eyes fixed on Jesus who had to run this race before us. We are to be motivated by His example. His eyes were always on the finish line and the joy that was set before Him of providing salvation for mankind, for which He endured the cross. He finished His race and is now set down at the right hand of God. He is our example and we are to follow in His footsteps in not growing weary and losing heart.

Demons recognize Christ's supreme authority over them (Mark 1:23-24; James 2:19) and believers share in this authority.

I Samuel 15:26-28 and 16:1-17 give us a foreshadow of Christ's victory on the cross. Saul was stripped of his kingdom and David was anointed king by God, but still Saul acted as king though rejected by God while David was the truly Divinely recognized king. Samuel told king Saul "the Lord has torn the kingdom of Israel from you today and given it to one of your neighbors – to one better than you" (I Samuel 15: 28). Then Samuel went and anointed David. "So Samuel took the horn of oil and anointed him in the presence of his brothers, and from that day on the Spirit of the Lord came upon David in power" (I Samuel 16:13).

We see that king Saul, while still recognized as king and acting as king, had been rejected by God, while David was recognized as king by God. But David waited for God's timing. While David was an outcast in the cave of Adullam, those who chose David over Saul gathered to him. If we have desires and longings that nothing in this world can satisfy, it is because we were created for another world and another love that alone can bring us fulfillment.

So too, Jesus is an outcast in this world (the Satanic realm) and those who feel a yearning for something beyond this world find their fulfillment in Christ. He gives us an essential purpose and meaning to our existence. He embraces us and assures us "Do not be afraid, I have overcome the world, I have defeated Satan. He has no more claim on you, I have paid for your sins and redeemed your life and now you belong to me."

Thus, we see that while Christ is victorious and now holds the title deed of the world, Satan still runs free, seeming to hold on to his authority. However, through the victory of the cross, Jesus is receiving those who have joined with Him and recognize Him as rightful Lord, those who are willing to serve Him and live as outcasts, while waiting for Him to receive His kingdom and return.

When the victorious Israelites entered Canaan, the promised land, under Joshua, they still had to take possession and reap the result of their victory. The experiences of Israel in its promised land is a foreshadow, or type, or example of the spiritual experiences of the believer in Christ.

For Israel, as they entered the land God had given them, the enemy still possessed it and did everything in its power to prevent them from reaping the benefits of the victory that God had given them. For believers in Christ, they may have entered into a new life from God, but the enemy, the spiritual forces arrayed against God's people, is determined to minimize the results of Christ's victory in the world. God has called His people to complete His victory wrought by Christ in Christ's power through the Holy Spirit. The end result of this is that the Christian's life becomes a warfare.

Every sinner who comes to Christ is removed from Satan's kingdom and transferred into Christ's kingdom and the victory of the cross is magnified. While Satan continues to be the prince of the world, Christ has won the victory over Satan and those who belong to Christ share in this victory. While Satan was defeated at the cross, the carrying out of his total destruction is yet in the future.

In the meantime, the spiritual forces of darkness are working to render Christ's work on the cross ineffective for as many as possible. Now that Satan's doom has been assured, he has intensified his warfare. Since the coming of Christ, Satan has waged uninterrupted warfare against believers, seducing them to neglect the work that Christ called them to do.

Because of the believer's total identification with Christ, whatever is true of Him is also true of the believer. Christ is now seated on the throne of heaven at the Father's right hand, the place of power and authority with the title deed of the kingdom, and the believer is seated there with Him. He has delegated to us the use of His authority. This is why we are exhorted to "submit yourselves then to God. Resist the devil, and he will flee from you" (James 4:7).

As there was a period between David's anointing and the final stripping of all authority from Saul, so too there is a period of time between Christ's total victory over Satan and when the final sentence is carried out. In the meantime, believers must realize that sitting in our comfortable pews while singing *Onward Christian Soldiers* and *Have Thine Own Way Lord* is not enough. We are called to proclaim the "Good News" that Christ has conquered death and hell, and now calls us back into fellowship with the One we were created for. Christ has removed the sin barrier between God and us, and now we can go home to Him one day.

CHAPTER 6
GOD'S FULL ARMOR

Today we are engaged in a spiritual war against a vicious and cruel pantheon of spiritual hosts of wickedness under the authority of the powerful and crafty prince of darkness whose methods are lies and deception. It is necessary to put on the full armor of God, "For our struggle is not against flesh and blood, but against the rulers, against the authorities, against the powers of this dark world and against the spiritual forces of evil in the heavenly realms" (Ephesians 6:12).

Paul describes the Christian life in terms of spiritual military service. He exhorts believers: "Endure hardship with us like a good soldier of Jesus Christ. No one serving as a soldier gets involved in civilian affairs – he wants to please his commanding officer" (II Timothy 2:4). We are to "fight the good fight of faith" (I Timothy 1:18; 6:12). We are to "wage war" (II Corinthians 10:3). We are to struggle with hardship and do without many human necessities because we "Can do everything through Him who gives me strength" (Ephesians 6:12-13).

When Paul wrote his letter to the Ephesians, he would have had a good knowledge of the pieces of Roman soldiers' armor from seeing it at close range while he was in a Roman prison guarded by Roman soldiers. Rome had the finest army in the world at the time, and Paul used it as an illustration of the armor that God has provided for His people in their warfare with Satan and his demons.

"Finally, be strong in the Lord and in His mighty power. Put on the full armor of God so that you can take your stand against the devil's schemes. For our struggle is not against flesh and blood, but against the rulers, against the authorities, against the powers of this dark world and against the spiritual forces of evil in the heavenly realms. Therefore put on the full armor of God, so that when the day of evil comes, you may be able to stand your ground, and after you have done everything, to stand" (Ephesians 6:10-13).

We see here that the Christian life is to be viewed as a *struggle*. Life for the believer is a continual warfare, and all believers must understand this and come to grips with spiritual reality. There are no days off, no vacations, no breaks, no recesses, but only an unending struggle with ceaseless, tireless, determined, supernatural forces "in the heavenly realms." This does not refer to some far off distant sphere, but rather to the invisible dimension, the unseen realities of the spirit world.

Because the enemy is unseen, this life for believers can be compared to driving an airplane in very bad weather. Make no mistake about it, we can become disoriented by the master deceiver. We cannot depend on our own understanding, in which case it is crucial that we go by the plane's instruments, which in our case is the Bible.

Our conflict with Satan and his demons brings us into a realm beyond human resources, and we must depend on our supernatural resources. The Bible is our infallible guide in times of confusion and fear. We are instructed to "Trust in the Lord with all your heart and lean not on your own understanding." We cannot depend on our own flawed human reasoning; we must put our trust in God's Word. If we do that, we have His promise: "In all your ways acknowledge Him, and He will make your paths straight" (Proverbs 3:5).

Through his hosts of evil spirits, Satan makes his assault on our lives. He works through *schemes*, which means devious plots, trickery, and deceptive assaults.

During everyday life, he sends his "fiery darts" which are evil suggestions to pull us away from our walk with the Lord.

Our confrontation with the supernatural powers under Satan arrayed against us is the very result of our belonging to Christ. This is what it is all about. Our wrestling against the hosts of wickedness is based on the foundation of the victory over Satan that Christ accomplished on the cross, "when God raised Him from the dead and seated Him at His right hand in the heavenly realms, far above all rule and authority, power and dominion, and every title that can be given, not only in the present age but also in the one to come. And God placed all things under His feet and appointed Him to be head over everything for the church, which is His body, the fullness of Him who fills everything in every way" (Ephesians 1:19-23).

The exaltation of the Head also exalted us, His body, as co-sharers in all that God has done with Christ, so that we are seated together with Him in the heavenly realms. This means that everything God did for the Head He did for the body as well. This means that positionally we are in the heavenly realms with our Head: "For you died, and your life is now hidden with Christ in God" (Colossians 3:3). Satan is a defeated enemy; his head was crushed at Calvary. We do not need to fight FOR victory, because already: "In all these things we are more than conquerors through Him who loved us" (Romans 8:37). We are to simply enter into the victory that Christ has already won for us.

Our fight is FROM Christ's victory that He won for us through His death and resurrection, on to victory after victory in His resurrection power. We died with Christ and rose with Him and now we are to live in His resurrection life. In Ephesians 1:18-23, Paul prays that God "may give you the spirit of wisdom and revelation that you may know Him better. I pray also that the eyes of your heart may be enlightened in order that you may know the hope to which He has called you, the riches of His glorious inheritance in the saints, and His incomparably great power for us who believe. That power is like the working of His mighty strength, which He exerted in Christ when He raised Him from the dead and seated Him at His right hand in the heavenly realms. Far above all rule and authority, power and dominion, and every title that can be given, not only in the present age but also in the one to come. And God placed all things under His feet and appointed Him to be head over everything for the church, which is His body, the fullness of Him who fills everything in every way."

In verse 18a we read that the eyes of the believer's heart may be enlightened. The heart refers to the whole inward man being overflowed with divine light so that these truths may be grasped. The purpose of the Holy Spirit's *enlightening* is to give us Spiritual insight, a clear understanding by experience of what He has revealed in His Word. "The hope to which He has called you," is the high calling to die to self and live for God through Christ. It is a call to be with Christ and ultimately to be like Christ.

Paul also prays that we may understand "The riches of His glorious inheritance in the saints" (Ephesians 1:18b). God can create anything at will, including angels, by simply speaking the word, but He does not create redeemed sinners in that way. They must be washed in the blood of His Son. These are His most precious possession, the pearl of great price, the church. These are the trophies of His grace that will be on display forever: "And God raised us up in Christ and seated us with Him in the heavenly realms in Christ Jesus, in order that in the coming ages he might show His incomparable riches of His grace, expressed in His kindness to us in Christ Jesus" (Ephesians 2: 6-7).

The Scriptures tell the story of God's eternal purpose to have an eternal companion for His Son. This eternal companion is described by John in the Book of Revelation as "the bride, the wife of the Lamb" (Revelation 21:9), who will share Christ's throne: "To him who overcomes, I will give the right to sit with Me on my throne, just as I overcame and sat down with My Father on His throne" (Revelation 3: 21).

The apostle Paul wrote in II Corinthians 11:3, "But I am afraid that just as Eve was deceived by the serpent's cunning, your minds may somehow be led astray from your sincere and pure devotion to Christ." Note two words in this verse. (1) "Deceived." The devil attempts to deceive us by mixing truth with error until we don't know the difference. To be deceived is to believe a lie. (2) The second word is "Cunning." This refers to shrewdness in manipulation – clever tricks, schemes and strategies. He doesn't attack us head on but finds an opening, a point of weakness, and continually attacks until our will is corrupted and breaks down.

The person who is corrupted or seduced by a temptation follows his own passions and desires rather than the will of God. Satan is very subtle and seductive to step-by-step draw us away from God toward the fulfillment of our fleshly desires.

Colossians 3:1-3 tells us, "Since, then, you have been raised with Christ, set your hearts on things above, where Christ is seated at the right hand of God. Set your mind on things above, not on earthly things. For you died and your life is now hidden with Christ in God." Christ's work on Calvary has placed us far above all principalities and powers, and our victory over the enemy begins from that position.

Paul says that the believer is to "Be strong in the Lord and in His mighty power" (Ephesians 6:10). This mighty power is Christ's victory at Calvary, made a living reality in our lives by the Holy Spirit. The office of the Holy Spirit is to take the things of Christ and make them a reality in our lives. These divine realities are manifested to us as we walk in the Holy Spirit.

The working of the Holy Spirit is inseparable from Christ's victory on the cross. This is the unmovable foundation of the work of the Holy Spirit. It was there that Christ disarmed the satanic powers and authorities "triumphing over them by the cross" (Colossians 2:15). The Holy Spirit's work is to apply to the believer the victory of Calvary by baptizing us into Christ's death and resurrection and bringing us into union with Him in His resurrection life.

The Holy Spirit is also the power that makes the believer's witness of the cross a mighty weapon for the pulling down of Satan's strongholds. Without this, our witnessing is lifeless and unproductive. Mere arguments and reasoning in our own power will have no effect against the spiritual forces arrayed against us. Only by the victory of Calvary through the Holy Spirit can we know victory over the powers of darkness.

"Put on the full armor of God" (Eph. 6:10-11) so that when the day of battle with evil comes you may be able to hold your ground against the devil's assault, and after holding your ground, you will still be standing ready for the next assault.

Paul uses highly figurative language. These pieces of spiritual armor are not literal entities in themselves but are symbols that represent what is real. The armor is symbolic of the Lord Jesus Christ and His work on the cross on our behalf. Romans 13:14 shows us this truth: "Put on the Lord Jesus Christ, and do not think about how to gratify the desires of the sinful nature."

"Stand firm then, with the belt of truth buckled around your waist, with the breastplate of righteousness in place, and with your feet fitted with the readiness that comes from the gospel of peace. In addition to all this, take up the shield of faith, with which you can extinguish all the flaming arrows of the evil one. Take the helmet of salvation and the sword of the Spirit, which is the Word of God. And pray in the Spirit on all occasions with all kinds of prayers and requests. With this in mind, be alert and always keep on praying for all the saints" (Ephesians 6: 14-18).

The first piece in the believer's armor is the "belt of truth" (verse 14a). In the Roman armor, the belt was made of leather six to eight inches wide and covered with scales of copper or iron, and went around the waist and protected the groin. The soldiers wore short skirts or kilts. Over which they wore a long flowing cloak, which was held in place at the waist by this wide belt. When preparing for battle they would tuck the cloak up under the belt allowing the legs to move unhindered.

It was a vital piece of equipment because everything else was fastened to it, making the armor secure. A loose fitting armor would be very awkward and clumsy. The Christian's foundational piece of armor is Truth - a growing knowledge and understanding of the Scriptures and how they apply to our lives. The belt of truth must be in place and secure, or else nothing else will fit. Christ is the ultimate truth, the key to life, the ultimate reality. In Colossians 2:3, Paul speaks of "the full riches of complete understanding, in order that they may know the mystery of God, namely, Christ, in whom are hidden all the treasures of wisdom and knowledge."

Knowing the truth is vital in spiritual warfare because the Devil's main tactic is deception. He works through all kinds of clever lies and false views. He is a master at this. This is the battle for our minds. Satan's greatest fear is the Bible, the Word of God; because it exposes him and his methods, and reveals the weapons we have in Christ. Through false religion based on human reasoning, he blinds the minds of unbelievers to the gospel of Jesus Christ.

We have reached the time the Bible predicted would come: "For the time will come when men will not put up with sound doctrine. Instead to suit their own desires, they will gather around them a great number of teachers to say what there itching ears want to hear. They will turn their ears away from the truth and turn aside to myths" (II Timothy 4:3-4). And II Peter 2:1 also gives a prediction of the days we live in: "But there were also false prophets among the people, just as there will be false teachers among you. They will secretly introduce destructive heresies, even denying the sovereign Lord who bought them."

Here we are told that the devil's deceptions will lead to the denial of the truth that Satan hates above all others: that Christ purchased our salvation on the cross (John 3:16).

These fallen angels are malevolent beings whose shrewdness and cunning in dealing with mankind has developed over thousands of years. Mankind, unaided by God, is no match for them.

They have mastered the art of deceptive temptation, and to his great delight his advantage has been greatly increased by the fact that men have been duped into believing that he is a myth. He doesn't care how we view him as long as it does not come from the Bible.

"With the breastplate of righteousness in place" (verse 14b). The Roman breastplate was made of bronze backed with thick, tough pieces of hide which protected the vital organs, especially the heart and lungs from full penetration from knives and arrows. It was fastened to the belt. The breastplate of the believer is the righteousness of Christ applied to the believer: "God made Him who had no sin to be sin for us, so that in Him we might become the righteousness of God" (II Cor. 5:21).

We are not only forgiven all of our sins but we are clothed with Christ's righteousness. As far as God is concerned, believers are "in Christ" and God always deals with us from this perspective. The believer does not stand in his own righteousness but in the perfect righteousness of Christ and has full acceptance with God. It is vital that we have a thorough knowledge of the victory that Christ has won on our behalf. Through Him we have a perfect standing with God. This is positional righteousness. Righteousness that God puts on my legal record because of my faith in Christ.

Paul refers to righteous living as a result of Christ's righteousness being given to us, a practical righteousness. It is righteousness in everyday living, which is possible because of our positional righteousness in Christ.

CHAPTER 7
GOD'S FULL ARMOR 2

"And your feet fitted with the readiness that comes from the gospel of peace" (verse 15). The proper footwear is very important in warfare. The Roman soldier wore boots with thick soles with metal studs that enabled him to make long marches over hazardous terrain, and to keep his footing on uneven ground and slippery slopes and in hand- to-hand combat. They were light and flexible for quick movement when using the sword, and for speed on long marches to surprise the enemy. Sure footing is essential in warfare.

"The gospel of peace" is the good news of Christ's death and resurrection for our sins. Every Christian should be grounded in the fact that we have peace with God in our hearts and know that we are secure in Christ and should be ready to carry out our responsibility to witness the good news of the gospel to others. Before we can rescue others, we must first be sure of our own footing.

These gospel shoes are for both stability and endurance in warfare and swiftness in bringing the gospel to others. In Romans 10:15, Paul quotes from the prophets Isaiah and Nahum and gives God's definition: "How beautiful are the feet of those who bring good news." The word *gospel* is from the Greek word *evangelion* from which we get our word *evangelism*, meaning *good message* or *good news*.

Bringing the gospel to others is a vital part of our warfare against the demonic forces. Far too many Christians are not in a state of readiness to witness to the lost.

I Peter 3:15 exhorts us, "Always be ready to give an answer to everyone who asks you to give the reason for the hope that you have."

Unsaved people are held as prisoners in Satan's grip, and it is our duty to give them the message of deliverance through Christ. Every believer should be doing some form of missionary work in their own sphere of influence. They should have a prayer list that they pray over daily. This gives meaning and purpose to our lives.

Since we have peace with God, nothing else should disturb our peace. Satan is a defeated foe. All he has to bring against the believer is his growl to frighten us. Fear keeps us from taking decisive action that wins spiritual battles. Like David against Goliath, we are to go in the name of the Lord, knowing that Jesus has already defeated him and that "the one who is in you is greater than the one who is in the world" (I John 4:4). We can face whatever comes our way with the assurance of our relationship with Christ and that nothing can destroy that relationship.

However, while Satan cannot destroy our relationship with Christ, he can break our fellowship with Christ and our effectiveness for Christ. His goal is to keep us from winning people to Christ. Jesus warned that there would be great conflict in our witnessing to the gospel, "I am sending you out like sheep among wolves" (Matthew 10:16); "a man's enemies will be the members of his own household" (Matthew 10:36). They must expect persecution even from their friends and family members (Matthew 10:34-36). He announces that He came to bring bloodshed (a sword). It is not His followers that would practice violence, but they were to expect violence to be done to them. We are seeing this happening around the world.

Satan continues to come after us and seek every way possible to undermine what we say and do so that our influence for Christ will be ineffective. It is for this reason he continues to pursue us and use all his deceptive strategies to discourage us and fill us with doubts and depression and make our lives miserable. He seeks to draw us away from God. That always has been his ultimate goal. He wants to get us off track from the will of God.

God's Word commands us to resist the devil. These pieces of armor are an acknowledgment of God's power and authority. In Ephesians 6:10-14, Paul repeatedly uses words and phrases of resistance: "So that you can take your stand" (vs. 11); "Stand your ground" (vs. 13); "Stand firm" (vs. 14). We are to stand firm on what Jesus has already accomplished on our behalf. That means resisting the devil's attacks and temptations and refusing to give up on what God wants to accomplish in our lives.

We are to stand firm in the finished work of Christ and withstand Satan's clever temptations that are aimed to entice us and knock us off balance and move us to partake of things that are contrary to His purpose for us. How we respond to the enemy's attacks determines whether our faith will be strengthened or weakened. In the book of James we read, "Submit yourselves, then, to God. Resist the devil, and he will flee from you" (4:7). In First Peter we read, "Be self-controlled and alert. Your enemy the devil prowls around like a roaring lion looking for someone to devour. Resist him, standing firm in the faith . . ." (5: 8-9).

He devours his victims through lies and deception, which leads to our next piece of armor: "In addition to all this, take up the shield of faith with which you can extinguish all the flaming arrows of the evil one" (verse 16).

The Roman shield was made of wood and covered with leather and metal. The Romans had two types of shields. One was small and round and was worn on the arm for hand-to-hand combat. The other type, the one described here is the *door shield*. It was used in open fighting. It was big and covered the soldier's body.

It was designed to be drenched with water so it could withstand the flaming arrows that were dipped in pitch and lit on fire. Any thought or impulse that entices us toward sin is a *flaming arrow*. "For everything in the world – the cravings of sinful man, the lusts of the eyes and the boasting of what he has and does – does not come from the Father but from the world" (I John 2:16).

The battlefield is in the mind. Temptations and doubts and pride all begin in the mind. Our actions follow the thoughts of the mind. The mind forms our decisions. It is with our minds that we evaluate the truth from fiction and make choices. Satan sends thoughts. A thought itself is not a sin; it is what we do with these thoughts that matters. It is our minds that motivate our wills. It is here that we are motivated to do our utmost for the Lord or to give up and give in to life's troubles. It is in our minds we develop our beliefs and attitudes that motivate what we say and do.

Satan knows our weaknesses; he also knows our strengths and our pride. I Corinthians 10:12 warns us, "So if you think you are standing firm, be careful that you don't fall!" It is our strong points that we take for granted. Many times in the Bible we read of great men of God snared by the devil in their strong point. We read in numbers 12:3 of Moses: "Now Moses was a very humble man, more humble than anyone else on the face of the earth."

In Exodus 17, Moses was told to strike the rock at Horeb and water would come out of it for the people to drink. The rock represented Christ who was struck on the cross, out of which came living water. But later on in Numbers 20:8, when the people were again in need of water, Moses was told to speak to the rock this time. But Moses became angry because of the complaining of the people and disobeyed God by taking his staff and striking the rock twice, thus disobeying God.

Again, the rock represented Christ who was struck once on the cross and needed only to be spoken to in order to deliver the water of life. I Corinthians 10:4 tells us that the rock represented Christ: "They drank from the same spiritual rock that accompanied them, and that rock was Christ." And because of his disobedience, Moses was not allowed to enter the Promised Land with the people. So Moses was tripped up by Satan in his strong point, His humility.

Peter's strong point was his boldness, and it is at this point he was tripped up by Satan when he denied the Lord three times out of fear (Luke 22:54-62).

It was the same with Elijah whose strongpoint was his faith and boldness. In I Kings 18:16-45 he challenged the prophets of Baal and brought down fire to consume the sacrifice on Mount Carmel and rout the false prophets of Baal. And James 5:17 tells us Elijah "prayed earnestly and it did not rain on the land for three and a half years. Again he prayed and the heavens gave rain, and the earth produced its crops."

But when Jezebel became enraged at what he did to her priests of Baal, she threatened to put him to death (I Kings 19: 1-13). Elijah became afraid and ran for his life. He sat down under a broom tree and prayed that he would die. Then he laid down and fell asleep and was touched by an angel who told him to get up and eat. The angel had brought him a "cake of bread" and a "jar of water."

When a soldier knelt down and held this shield over him, he was fully protected. This is how faith in the sense of confidence and trust operates. Like David when he went out to fight Goliath with trust not in himself but in the living God, when the evil one fires thoughts or doubts into our minds, our faith quenches those thoughts.

This is our most powerful defensive weapon against the enemy. Faith has nothing to do with feelings or outward appearances. True faith rests upon the Word of God. It is simply the belief that God will do what He says in His Word. Christ has won the victory, and those who place their faith in Him win the victory too. "For everyone born of God overcomes the world. This is the victory that has overcome the world, even our faith" (I John 5: 4).

This does not mean we will not be tested to the limit. Even though Joseph was to be used by God for a special purpose, God allowed his brothers to throw him into a pit and sold into slavery and carried off to Egypt, where he was falsely accused by his owner and thrown into a dungeon. But our faith enables us understand that no matter how severe the trial, God is in control and our trial will be limited to what we can bear in its severity and its duration. And we can expect to be stronger after we have been tested to the limit of our endurance. Our faith will determine if the trial weakens or strengthens our faith.

Unbelief is the root cause of all our evils. This fiery dart was first planted in the heart of our first parents and established Satan's power in the world and turned our Eden into a barren desert. Hebrews 12:1 refers to the sin "that so easily entangles us." Hebrews Chapter 11 shows that this sin that "so easily entangles us" is unbelief. One of the greatest problems in a believer's life is unbelief. In order to withstand the assaults of unbelief, we must learn to use the shield of faith to quench the fiery arrows of doubt that Satan and his cohorts, the evil spirits, are flinging at us.

We must keep our eyes on Jesus in order to walk on the water of our circumstances. If we take our eyes off of Jesus, the waters become storm tossed raging billows causing us to doubt. How often Jesus must say to us, "You of little faith, why did you doubt?" In Genesis 1:15, God said to Abraham, "Do not be afraid Abraham, I am your shield, your very great reward." Faith here is reliance upon and implicit trust in the Person of God and His trustworthiness.

The next piece of equipment is to protect our head or mind: "take the helmet of salvation" (verse 17a). This protects our thought lives from the enemy's lies and enables us to see life from the perspective of eternity. Roman helmets were made of leather with plates of metal at the temples and forehead.

In spiritual warfare, it is vital that the believer is secure in his own salvation. We must be able to say with Paul, "I know whom I have believed, and am convinced that he is able to guard what I have entrusted to Him for that day."

Satan is always alert to take advantage of each situation with the specific purpose of taking our minds off God and His provisions for us. We remember that when Peter was walking on the water, he was doing great, while his eyes were on Jesus; but when he took his eyes off Jesus and focused his attention on the stormy sea, he began to sink. This lesson was given in Scripture for every believer. As we walk through our particular storms, we must keep the eyes of our faith focused on Jesus and His ability to provide for us in the midst of our storms.

In spiritual warfare, the helmet of salvation protects the mind from false teaching and false views of God. Satan's foundational attack is on the Word of God. If we are confused on God's Word, then everything is in confusion. Satan's systematic attack always begins with God's Word. This deception began in the Garden of Eden. The helmet of salvation keeps our minds focused on the completion of our salvation and on the fact that we are to be working for that day when we will stand before God.

In I Thessalonians 5:8, it is called the "hope of salvation." As believers, we are now saved from the penalty of sin and look forward to being saved from the presence of sin in our new sinless bodies.

While the believer is saved now, he looks forward to the completion of his salvation at the rapture and resurrection of believers, when Christ comes for us and takes us to the Father house (John 14:1-4). The word *hope* here is not used in the sense that we hope it will happen but maybe it won't, but in the sense of assurance for something we are still waiting for.

Philippians 1:6 refers to both present and future aspects of our salvation: "Being confident of this, that He who began a good work in you (when we believed the gospel) will carry it on to completion until the day of Jesus Christ," (when believers are glorified).

"And the sword of the Spirit which is the Word of God" (verse 17b). The Romans used a short sword, only about 18 to 24 inches long and sharpened on both sides (a double-edged sword) so that no matter which way it was swung, it was lethal.

This Roman sword was the ultimate weapon in the ancient world. It revolutionized ancient warfare. A trained soldier could fight from any position so the soldier was never off balance. The opposing soldiers used much larger swords and had to get in position and needed room to swing. The Roman soldier would step inside, too close for the enemy to use his longer sword, making his weapon useless and quickly finishing him off.

In the spiritual realm, the Word of God is our only offensive weapon and it is the only one we need for defeating the satanic forces arrayed against us. There are two Greek terms used for *Word*. One is *logos* and refers to the complete revelation of God. The second term is used here; it is the word *rhema* and refers to a specific *saying of God*, a verse or passage of Scripture, and refers to a specific application to an immediate situation. It is a *saying of God* applied to a specific temptation. The Bible is filled with *sayings of God* and they are all doubled-edged. The Bible is God's arsenal filled with double-edged swords.

Here the *Word of God* is a saying applied to a certain situation. This is the weapon against which there is no defense. Christ is our example in the use of this weapon against the devil. His answer to every temptation was met with "it is written" (Matthew 4:4-11).

"For the Word of God is living and active. Sharper than any double-edged sword, it penetrates even to the dividing of soul and spirit, joints and marrow; it judges the thoughts and attitudes of the heart. Nothing in all creation is hidden from God's sight. Everything is uncovered and laid bare to the eyes of Him to whom we must give account" (Hebrews 4:12). The Word of God is living and active because it is energized and empowered by the Holy Spirit.

It is the only offensive weapon we need, and II Timothy 3:16-17 tells us why: "All Scripture is God-breathed and is useful for teaching, rebuking, correcting and training in righteousness, so that the man of God may be thoroughly equipped for every good work."

The breath of God refers to the Holy Spirit. The word *Spirit* has the meaning of *breath* or *wind* and refers to *lifeforce*. In the Hebrew it is *ruah*; in the Greek, *pneuma*. This is brought out in John 20:22: "And with that He (Jesus) breathed on them and said, 'Receive the Holy Spirit.'" And in Genesis 2:7, "The Lord God formed the man from the dust of the ground and breathed into his nostrils the breath of life, and the man became a living soul."

As God breathed life into the man He breathed out His life-giving Word in the Scriptures. The Holy Spirit presides in His Word. This is why the Scriptures can bring life (the new birth). The Holy Spirit is forever associated with the Word of God.

"For you have been born again, not of perishable seed, but of imperishable through the living and enduring Word of God. For 'All men are like grass, and all their glory is like the flowers of the field; the grass withers and the flowers fall, but the Word of the Lord stands forever.' And this was the Word that was preached to you" (I Peter 1: 23-25). "The Word of God is living and active," Luther said. "The Word of God has legs, it runs after me. The Word of God has hands, it lays hold of me."

But it is not enough to have the Word of God in our homes. It must be stored in our hearts to be used on the battlefield of our lives. Satan attacks our minds because he knows our minds direct our actions. God's answer is to saturate our minds with His Word, which penetrates all the enemy's deceptions and convicts us. His deceptions are revealed and cannot hide from God for God reveals them through His Word.

When Jesus was tempted in His humanity, His answer to every temptation was to quote the word of God, "It is written" (Matthew 4:4, 7, 10). Here Jesus demonstrated for us the use of the "sword of the Spirit" (Ephesians 6:17). In Matthew 4:4 Jesus quotes from Deuteronomy 8:3: "Man does not live by bread alone, but on every word (Greek rhema) that comes from the mouth of God." When the Scriptures refer to the word of God and uses the Greek logos, it refers to the Word of God in general, while the word *rhema* refers to a specific utterance or saying of God.

We must understand that when Jesus came in His humanity it was not to defeat the devil for himself. If this was merely a battle between Jesus and Satan, Jesus could have simply spoken the command and Satan would have been cast immediately into Hell. However Jesus came in His humanity to defeat the devil in our, His bride's, behalf.

Jesus not only came to suffer for our sins but also to show us how to live and use the weapons He won for us. In

His temptation Jesus was showing us how to use the sword of the Spirit. We are to use an appropriate saying of Scripture while depending on the Holy Spirit, its Author, to meet the specific temptation of Satan. This same weapon that Jesus used in His humanity to defeat Satan has also been given to us by God, making Jesus victory our victory.

Satan directs all his efforts to keep us unaware of the supernatural provisions God has made for our daily victory. This principle is important to remember. Christ empowers us to do whatever He commands us to do: "For it is God who works in you to will and to act according to His good purpose" (Philippians 2:13).

It is important to note that there is no armor for our backs, no protection if we turn and run from the enemy. If we cower from the evil one, we expose ourselves to his fiery missiles. There is no provision for retreating for the believer. We must face the enemy boldly in the power of the finished work of Christ.

"And pray in the Spirit on all occasions with all kinds of prayers and requests. With this in mind, be alert and always keep on praying for all the saints" (6:18).

We are to pray as directed by the Holy Spirit. Prayer is an essential connection in the working of God in this world. The Holy Spirit, the Author of Scripture, has revealed to us the prayers He will answer. The Father does not consent to answering anything we pray for. No father would be so gullible. God has made promises and these form the requests that God has promised to answer.

To "pray in the Spirit" is to pray according to the promises the Spirit has given in the Scriptures. These are His revealed will, and elsewhere we are promised that God will answer prayer according to His will (I John 5:14

Satan is constantly observing us, waiting for us to let our armor slip, giving him the slightest opening to fling in his flaming arrows.

CHAPTER 8
THE DEVIL'S NAMES AND TITLES AND HIS CHARACTER

He is called Satan, which means Adversary. He is opposed to God. He is for anything that grieves God and degrades mankind. He has been influential in all the sin and corruption and hate and horror of mankind's brutal history.

He is referred to as the *Devil* or *slanderer* (Revelation 12:10; see Job 1:16 and Zechariah 3:1). He slanders God before the world. He started with Adam and Eve by calling God a liar and deceiver (Genesis 3: 4-5). He uses this tactic on believers as well as unbelievers. In Revelation 12:10, he is called the accuser of believers. He accuses believers before God day and night. He is constantly pointing out our failures to God, While Jesus defends believers on the basis of His shed blood (I John 2: 1-2).

He is *the god of this age.* "The god of this age has blinded the minds of unbelievers, so that they cannot see the light of the gospel of the glory of Christ who is the image of God" (II Corinthians 4:4). He controls the world-system, or mindset against God: "We know that we are the children of God, and that the whole world (this world-system) is under the control of the evil one" (I John 5:19). In Luke 4:4-5, Satan said he would give Jesus the kingdoms of the world and their authority and splendor, "for it has been given to me, and I can give it to anyone I want to. So if you worship me, it will be yours." Jesus did not dispute His right to do this, but confirmed it by referring to him as the "prince of this world" (John 12:31; 14:30; 16:11).

"Has blinded the minds of unbelievers." Once men or woman receive enough light or understanding of their need of salvation and still refuse to believe (willful unbelief), then Satan blinds them to what they once understood. Romans 1:18-32 gives the account of mankind's rejection of the truth of God. Unregenerate mankind is under the wrath of God because they ignore the truth and are given over to wickedness. They are willfully blinded to what can be known about God. Through creation, His invisible attributes – His eternal power and Divine nature – can be clearly understood.

Mankind was created with an inner knowledge of the creator, and this understanding is confirmed by the creation, so men are without excuse. But they were deceived by Satan and believed his lie rather than the truth of the Living God, and their thinking became futile and their foolish hearts were darkened by the kingdom of darkness.

And in their pride they thought they were wise but became fools. They exchanged the glory of the immortal God for idols – images made to look like mortal man and birds and reptiles. As a result of this, God gave them over because they exchanged the truth of God for a lie and worshipped and served created things rather than the creator. And since they did not want to retain the knowledge of God, He gave them over to a depraved mind and allowed them to follow its evil desires.

When they forgot God, they forgot why they were created and lost purpose and meaning and became like beasts without a moral compass.

"Men loved darkness instead of light because their deeds were evil" (John 3:19). Man without the Spirit (the natural man, the fallen and unredeemed man) does not accept the things that come from the Spirit of God, for they are foolishness to him, and he cannot understand them, because they are Spiritually discerned (I Corinthians 2:14). And Satan who blinds sinners is ever ready to invalidate our witness while comforting the sinner in his rejection of Christ.

He is the "ruler of the kingdom of the air" (Ephesians 2: 2). As such he is the head of "The spiritual forces of evil in the heavenly realms" (Ephesians 6: 12) – "for our struggle is not against flesh and blood, but against the rulers, against the authorities, against the powers of this dark world and against the spiritual forces of evil in the heavenly realms."

HIS CHARACTER

He is proud and desires worship. The extent of this desire is seen in his attempt to have the Lord Jesus worship him (Luke 4:5-7). This desire will culminate in his being worshipped in the great tribulation through the antichrist (Revelation 13:4).

He is a liar and a murderer. He lied to Eve in the Garden that led to man's fall when he said, "You will not surely die" when she ate of the fruit of the tree (Gen 3:4). In John 8:44, Jesus said the devil was, "a murderer from the beginning, not holding to the truth, for there is no truth in him. When he lies, he speaks his native language, for he is a liar and the father of lies."

His lies are made more palatable by his appearing as an angel of light, along with his servants or ministers: "For such men are false apostles, deceitful workmen, masquerading as apostles of Christ. And no wonder for Satan himself masquerades as an angel of light. It is not surprising then, if his servants masquerade as servants of righteousness" (II Corinthians 11:13-15).

Satan's masterpieces of deception are ordained ministers and seminary professors who do not know God but claim to speak for Him. Men who, rather than teaching how to be right with God and fellowship with him, teach how to be rich and successful, or how to have great and proud self-esteem – a religion of humanism where man is God and true Bible-centered Christianity is mocked and ridiculed.

He is cruel as seen by the torment of those whom his demons possess and his overriding desire that men and women go to hell. He uses the world-system and false religion to keep their minds off of eternity. He not only influences false religions but also organized Christendom, or "churchianity" – the outward form or appearance of true Christianity: "Having a form of Godliness but denying its power" (II Cor. 3:5).

These churches have a form or appearance of Christianity but without its power of the Holy Spirit. They are unregenerate and spiritually dead. These ministers are emissaries of Satan who have disguised themselves as angels of light. In Matthew 13:37-43, Jesus explains the parable of the weeds: "He answered, 'the one who sowed the good seed is the Son of Man. The field is the world, and the good seed stands for the sons of the kingdom. The weeds are the sons of the evil one, and the enemy who sows them is the devil. The harvest is the end of the age, and the harvesters are angels.

'As the weeds are pulled up and burned in the fire, so it will be at the end of the age. The Son of Man will send His angels and they will weed out of His kingdom everything that causes sin and all who do evil. They will throw them into the fiery furnace, where there will be weeping and gnashing of teeth. Then the righteous will shine like the sun in the kingdom of their Father. He who has ears let him hear.'"

In this parable, we see that the devil sowed what closely resembled the genuine grain and that it was not until the time of harvest that one could be distinguished from the other; then it will be seen that the weeds, though appearing as wheat, bear no fruit. Here Satan uses the strategy of imitation. Satan's ministers look like the real thing. They do not appear as angels of darkness but as angels of light.

Satan has injected his deadly poison into the body of the organized church. Jesus sends out His servants while Satan sneaks his servants in among them, masquerading as ministers of light. The father of lies has cunningly changed the label on the bottle of poison to read *learning* and *scholarship*, undermining Biblical authority and creating what the apostle Paul calls "a different gospel – which is really no gospel at all" (Galatians 1: 6-7).

Paul goes on to say, "Evidently some people are throwing you into confusion and are trying to pervert the gospel of Christ. But even if we or an angel from heaven should preach a gospel other than the one we preached to you, let him be eternally condemned!" (Galatians 1: 6-8).

They are trying to sever the main artery of Christianity – Divine inspiration. God warns us of the secular humanizing of Christianity: "Turn away from godless chatter and the opposing ideas of what is falsely called knowledge, which some have professed and in so doing have wandered from the faith" (I Timothy 6:20-21). This refers to secular philosophies founded on the wisdom of this world.

CHAPTER 9
THE DEVIL'S POWER AND INFLUENCE AND METHODS

The Bible describes the angels as innumerable: "Then I looked and heard the voice of many angels, numbering thousands upon thousands and ten thousand times ten thousand (a hundred million)" (Rev. 5:11). Before he fell, Lucifer was the leader of a great number of angels who rebelled with him when he fell and constitute his army of fallen angels or demons. Revelation 12:4 tells us that a third of these angels followed Satan in his rebellion. These have been organized into a powerful hierarchy of principalities and powers of high-ranking demon princes: "For our struggle is not against flesh and blood but against the rulers, against the authorities, against the powers of this dark world and against the spiritual forces of evil in the heavenly realms" (Ephesians 6:12).

These "authorities" and "rulers are likened to generals and commanders of armies of mighty demonic forces. They are assigned to nations as well as individuals. Daniel 10:12-13 describes a powerful demon assigned to the kingdom of Persia, which today is Iran. Persia is specifically mentioned because they were the world rulers and ruled over Israel at the time. This demon was so powerful that he was able to hinder this angel from bringing the answer to Daniels prayer for 21 days, until Michael, the only angel with the designation of "archangel," (Jude 9) came to assist him.

This demon was called the "prince of Persia" and he was assigned to influence the Persian king against Israel.

Michael was assigned to offset the powerful influence of this angel. This angel tells Daniel that he had to return to continue fighting with the "prince of Persia" until the "prince of Greece" would come, when Greece under Alexander the Great would conquer the Persian Empire. Then the demon assigned to influence the Greek rulers against Israel would replace the prince of Persia.

The believer's battle is with the devil and his methods or strategies. Like a general, he organizes his forces. The "rulers," the "authorities," the "powers," and the "spiritual forces of evil" (Ephesians 6:12), are under his command. We are surrounded by a fearful and vast array of malignant and cruel soldiers of darkness – the aggressive warriors with whom we struggle.

Humans are also in Satan's service and are used by him to destroy our testimony and effectiveness for the Lord. Ultimately, our struggle is with mighty spiritual evil and invisible forces who motivate and influence the inhabitants of earth in a life and death struggle for heaven or hell, and mankind is the prize, for time and eternity.

He will do whatever it takes to stop believers from accomplishing God's will for our lives. He tempts us to do evil with cunning snares and fiery darts by suggesting evil thoughts: "And when the devil finished all his tempting, he left him until an opportune time" (Luke 4:13). "The evening meal was being served, and the devil had already prompted Judas Iscariot, son of Simon, to betray Jesus" (John 13:2). "Now a man named Ananias, together with his wife Sapphira, also sold a piece of property. With his wife's full knowledge he kept back part of the money for himself, but brought the rest and put it at the apostle's feet. Then Peter said, 'Ananias, how is it that Satan has so filled your heart that you have lied to the Holy Spirit and have kept for yourself some of the money you received for the land'" (Acts 5: 1-3).

He opposes the gospel: "Those along the path are the ones who hear, and then the devil comes and takes away the Word from their hearts, so that they may not be saved" (Luke 8:12). "The god of this age has blinded the minds of unbelievers so they cannot see the light of the gospel of Christ, who is the image of God" (II Corinthians 4:4).

"When anyone hears the massage about the kingdom and does not understand it, the evil one comes and snatches away what was sown in his heart" (Matthew 13:19).

He plants false prophets, unbelievers in the midst of believers (Matthew 13: 38-39): "The field is the world, and the good seed stands for the sons of the kingdom. The weeds are the sons of the evil one, and the enemy who sows them is the devil."

He hinders the work of believers (I Thessalonians 2:18). "Out of our intense longing, we made every effort to see you. For we wanted to come to you – certainly I, Paul, did, again and again – but Satan stopped us."

He transformed himself into a messenger of light, and he transforms some unbelievers into ministers of righteousness to deceive men (II Corinthians 11:14-15).

He energizes the unsaved: "As for you, you were dead in your transgressions and sins, in which you used to live when you followed the ways of this world and of the ruler of the kingdom of the air, the spirit who is now at work in those who are disobedient" (Ephesians 2:1-2).

He promotes the world-system: "We know that we are children of God and that the whole world is under the control of the evil one" (I John 5:19).

He deceives the whole world: "That ancient serpent called the devil or Satan, who leads the whole world astray" (Revelation 12: 9).

He accuses and slanders believers before God (Revelation 12:10): "For the accuser of our brothers, who accuses them before our God day and night, has been hurled down."

The believer's duty regarding Satan is to "Be self-controlled and alert. Your enemy the devil prowls around like a roaring lion looking for someone to devour. Resist him, standing firm in the faith, because you know that your brothers throughout the world are undergoing the same kinds of sufferings" (I Peter 5: 8-9). We must not allow Satan an opening to gain a foothold (Ephesians 4:27). We must "submit ourselves, then, to God. Resist the devil, and he will flee from you" (James 4:7).

We must ever be aware that Satan can only go as far as God will allow him to go in tempting us. We are promised "No temptation has seized you except what is common to man. And God is faithful; He will not let you be tempted beyond what you can bear. But when you are tempted, He will also provide a way out so that you can stand up under it" (1 Corinthians 10:13). God knows each of us and knows how much we can bear is ready to deliver us.

"We must not be unaware of His schemes" (II Corinthians 2:11). We must "put on the full armor of God so that you can take your stand against the devil's schemes" (Ephesians 6:11). We must overcome him by the Word of God (Matthew 4:1-11). We must "Live by the Spirit, and you will not gratify the desires of the sinful nature" (Galatians 5:16).

Satan is a defeated foe. He was defeated at the cross. We must constantly appropriate all that Christ won for us by His death and resurrection. We must follow Him in His triumphal march when He led captivity captive. I John 5:1 tells us, "This is the victory that overcomes the world, even our faith." We are to stand firm in our faith with the certain understanding that the battle is the Lord's. Our faith in His victory, already accomplished, is what overcomes the world.

This battle will continue to the end of the age: "Then the dragon was enraged at the woman and went off to make war with the rest of her offspring – those who obey God's commandments and hold to the testimony of Jesus" (Rev. 12:17). The children of the kingdom are those who trust in Christ. "You are all the children of God through faith in Jesus Christ (Gal. 3:26). The children of the serpent are those who reject Christ: "You brood of vipers . . ." (Matthew 12:34). "You snakes! You brood of vipers! How will you escape being condemned to hell" (Matthew 23:33).

"You belong to your father, the devil . . ." (John 8:44). In this struggle the seed of the woman would crush the serpent's head with a fatal deathblow, and "destroy the devil's work" (I John 3:8). But in the process of crushing the serpent's head with His heel, He would have to expose His heel to the serpent's deadly fangs.

God has an eternal plan for this world. This earth, the scene of the fall, would be the scene of the cosmic war where evil will be defeated. The "offspring of the woman" would be a second Adam to raise up humanity that the first Adam had brought down in the fall.

The climax of this struggle would take place on the cross. Satan would be utterly defeated at the cross, but it would cost the Son of God great agony and death. Because of Christ's victory on the cross, Jesus will ultimately crush Satan under the feet of His people: "The God of peace will soon crush Satan under your feet" (Rom. 16:20). But Jesus would have to give His life as a ransom to buy His people out of the slave market of sin.

The believer must be aware of the consequences of this warfare and be willing to endure hardship like a good soldier of Jesus Christ and not get involved in things that will take us away from the battlefield (II Timothy 2: 3-4). As Soldiers of Jesus Christ, we must be disciplined and ready for self-denial and hardship, for the battle will take courage and endurance, and will call for strength beyond mere human strength, as Paul exhorts us in Ephesians 6:10: "Finally, be strong in the Lord and in the power of His might."

The same world that hates Christ will also hate the believer in whom Christ dwells: "Do not be surprised, my brothers, if the world hates you" (I John 3:13). The world here refers to the satanic controlled system: "How great is the love the Father has lavished upon us, that we should be called the children of God. And that is what we are! The reason the world (the satanic-system) does not know us is that it did not know Him" (I John 3:1).

Satan's great desire, which was the first sin, is given in Isaiah 14:14: "I will make myself like the most high." It is seen again in his temptation of Eve in Genesis 3:5: "You will be like God." And when he met Jesus as the Last Adam in Luke 4:7: "If you worship me."

His great desire is still to take the place of God. We finally see this all-consuming desire of his in the antichrist who, "Will oppose and will exalt himself over everything that is called God or is worshipped, so that he sets himself up in God's temple, proclaiming himself to be God" (II Thessalonians 2:4).

This will take place during the tribulation period when Satan is cast down to the earth: "And there was war in heaven. Michael and his angels fought against the dragon, and the dragon and his angels fought back. But he was not strong enough, and they lost their place in heaven. The great dragon was hurled down – that ancient serpent called the devil, or Satan, who leads the whole world astray. He was hurled to the earth and his angels with him" (Revelation 12:7-9).

Jude 6 describes certain fallen angels as being kept in darkness and bound with chains for judgment as soon as they fell. So certain fallen angels or demons were so bad that they were bound immediately to be released as part of the judgment of the great tribulation.

The place they were bound seems to be the bottomless pit or Abyss of revelation 9:1-3, 11, where they are kept to be released during the tribulation period. In these three verses we read: "The fifth angel sounded his trumpet, and I saw a star that had fallen from the sky to the earth. The star was given the key to the shaft of the Abyss. When he opened the Abyss, smoke rose from it like the smoke of a gigantic furnace. The sun and sky were darkened by the smoke from the Abyss. And out of the smoke locusts came down upon the earth and were given power like that of scorpions of the earth" (Revelation 9:1-3). "They had as king over them, the angel of the Abyss, whose name in Hebrew is Abaddon, and in Greek Apollyon" (Revelation 9:11). Here Abaddon and Apollyon mean *Destroyer* and refers to Satan.

Angels will accompany our Lord at His second coming: "When the Son of Man comes in His glory, and all the angels with Him, He will sit on His throne of heavenly glory" (Revelation 25: 31).

Satan will be bound for the thousand year millennium: "And I saw an angel coming down out of heaven, having the key to the abyss and holding in his hand a great chain. He seized the dragon, that ancient serpent, who is the devil or Satan. And bound him for a thousand years. He threw him into the abyss, and locked and sealed it over him, to keep him from deceiving the nations anymore until the thousand years were ended. After that he must be set free for a short time" (Revelation 20:1-3).

Angels will separate unsaved mankind from Christ's kingdom: "The Son of Man will send out His angels and they will weed out of His kingdom everything that causes sin and all who do evil" (Matthew 13:41).

Satan will be cast into the Lake of Fire: "And the devil, who deceived them, was thrown into the lake of burning sulfur, where the beast and the false prophet had been thrown. They will be tormented day and night for ever and ever" (Revelation 20:10). He will not be the lord of hell but will suffer the same judgment as those he has seduced.

HIS METHODS

"The Spirit clearly says that in the latter times some will abandon the faith and follow deceiving spirits and things taught by demons" (I Tim 4:1). Satan's supreme goal is to influence the Church, not to destroy it, but control it and pervert its purpose. His goal is for a large church whose members are spiritually dead. A building filled with worldly learning, with money and influence and more concern about social standing than about a relationship with God: "Deceiving spirits and things taught by demons."

The apostle Peter warns us: "But there were also false prophets among the people, just as there will be false teachers among you. They will secretly introduce destructive heresies, even denying the sovereign Lord who bought them" (II Pet. 2:1). Jesus warned us that Satan was "a murderer from the beginning, not holding to the truth, for there is no truth in him. When he lies he speaks his native language, for he is a liar and the father of lies" (John 8:44).

Satan's cleverest deceptions sound like the truth. His most effective work will be done in the church. Since Satan's greatest concern is to blind men and women to their need of the gospel, much of his activity centers on hindering the ministry of believers. Where the kingdom of God is being spread, the kingdom of darkness will be most active.

His methods are deception and distortion, by masquerading as an angel of light, by counterfeiting. This is what Paul calls, "The schemes of the devil" in Ephesians 6:11. He uses deception, sets traps and snares, promotes illusions and generally keeps pounding away at us until we give in to him. Then he builds a stronghold of defeatism until we give up ever winning, and keeps us in an attitude of weakness and defeat. Our best protection against the wiles of the devil comes from knowledge of the Bible.

"For the Word of God is living and active. Sharper than any double-edged sword, it penetrates even to dividing soul and spirit, joints and marrow. It judges the thoughts and attitudes of the heart. Nothing in all of creation is hidden from God's sight. Everything is uncovered and laid bare before the eyes of Him to whom we must give account" (Heb. 4:12-13).

The Word of God is powerful; it is alive and active. It reveals the thoughts and attitudes of the heart. Nothing is hidden from God; everything is exposed to God, the Author of Scripture. All the devil's tricks and snares and clearly laid out in God's Word.

II Corinthians 10:4-5 tells us, "The weapons we fight with are not the weapons of the world. On the contrary, they have divine power to demolish strongholds. We demolish arguments and every pretension that sets itself up against the knowledge of God, and we take captive every thought to make it obedient to Christ."

Arguments here refer to false speculations and false philosophies against God – false doctrines and wrong beliefs that call into question what God has said in the Scriptures. We are to bring these "into captivity to the obedience of Christ." We are to take captive and cast out every thought that is contrary to God's Word. We are to bring our thoughts into agreement with Christ's teachings.

Satan seeks to get us to think wrong thoughts about God, to be suspicious and critical of God's Word. This was His method with Eve to get her to doubt God's word and His goodness. We are to do what Jesus did against him, simply use the Scriptures – the sword of the Spirit.

To do this, it is vital that we read, study, meditate, and memorize the Word of God until it is a normal part of our thinking for effective use. Along with the Scriptures, we must add watchful prayer. When we neglect prayer, we become more anxious and fretful about things. We carry our burdens in our own strength, which we were never meant to do. We will soon become overwhelmed with fears and anxieties, and we will lose motivation to do God's will.

Our trust and confidence in God will wane and we will depend on our own resources, which soon fail; and we will leave off reading the Bible, praying, and witnessing. This is Satan's goal: to leave us spiritually paralyzed and ineffective until we begin to think in terms of defeat and lose all ambition to do God's will. In trusting prayer, we lean on God to take care of every aspect of our lives. This gives our lives confidence and power to do God's will. The believer who is convinced of God's love and care for him or her gives the devil heartburn.

CHAPTER 10
THE WORLD

His two means of reaching us are through the world (satanic-system) and the flesh (the fallen nature, the sin nature). He is constantly sending out his propaganda that happiness lies in freedom to enjoy the things God forbids. He is constantly trying to pull us off of our Biblical foundation.

There are two uses of the word *world* in Scripture. One is the physical planet we live on, and the other refers to the world-system of demonic influence and control that is opposed to God. This is the meaning when the word is used in a moral sense. The whole cosmos or world-system is under the delusion of the Satanic deception or blindness and, of course, is unaware of what they are blinded to – the saving gospel of Jesus Christ.

"The god of this age has blinded the minds of unbelievers so that they cannot see the light of the gospel of the glory of Christ, who is the image of God" (II Corinthians 4:4). "When anyone hears the message about the kingdom and does not understand it, the evil one comes and snatches away what was sown in the heart" (Matt. 13:19).

This is why Jesus said: "I have come into the world as a light, so that no one who believes in me should stay in darkness" (John 12:46); and why He said of believers, "They are not of this world (cosmos), even as I am not of the world (cosmos)" (John 17:14), and "In the world (cosmos) you will have trouble. But take heart! I have overcome the world (cosmos)" (John 16:33).

"We know that we are children of God, and that the whole world is under the control of the evil one" (I John 5:19).

"The world (cosmos) through its wisdom did not know Him (God)" (1 Corinthians 1:21).

"The world (cosmos) does not know you (the Father)" (John 17:25).

"My kingdom is not of this world (cosmos)" (John 18:36).

Believers are exhorted to "keep one self from being polluted by the world (cosmos)" (James 1:27).

The cosmos is the world-system promoted by Satan with his ideals and goals that began at the tower of Babel recorded in Genesis 11 as a tower or ziggurat (a brick platform shaped like a pyramid reaching toward heaven to worship the planets and stars) and it will culminate in the antichrist: "Men worshipped the dragon, because he had given authority to the beast and they also worshipped the beast" (Revelation 13: 4).

Satan is working toward a one-world government that will be empowered by him in the person of the antichrist. It will be Satan's imitation of Christ's kingdom that will promote universal worship through the antichrist. In Daniel chapters 2 and 7, Daniel has a vision of four beasts representing the four world-empires that would dominate the world throughout history. These were Babylon followed by Medo-Persia, Greece, and finally Rome. The fourth empire is the Roman in its two forms – that of past history and again in its future revived form.

Daniel asks for an explanation of the fourth beast. In Daniel 7:23 we read, "He gave me this explanation; the fourth beast is a fourth kingdom that will appear on earth. It will be different from all the other kingdoms, and will devour the whole earth, trampling it down and crushing it."

The past Roman Empire conquered much of the known world surrounding the Mediterranean, including much of Africa, Asia, and Europe, but not the entire world. It will be the Roman Empire in its revived form, prior to the return of Christ, that will "devour the whole earth" during the great tribulation.

Before that happens, the rapture of believers must take place. The believer is a citizen of heaven: "But our citizenship is in heaven" (Philippians 3:20). "Rejoice that your names are written in heaven" (Luke 10:20). Believers are citizens of heaven with their names written on its citizenship roll.

Antichrist will come to power at the beginning of the tribulation period, coinciding with the time when the Holy Spirit ceases His work of restraining sin in the world and its tendency toward antichrist, referred to in II Thessalonians 2:7: "For the secret power of lawlessness is already at work; but the one who now holds it back will continue to do so till he be taken out of the way." He will be controlled and empowered by Satan beyond any other in history.

Revelation 12:7-9 reads, "And there was war in heaven. Michael and his angels fought against the dragon, and the dragon and his angels fought back. But he was not strong enough and they lost their place in heaven. The great dragon was hurled down – that ancient serpent called the devil, or Satan, who leads the whole world astray. He was hurled down to the earth and his angels with him."

Revelation 12:12 adds, "Therefore rejoice, you heavens and you who dwell in them! But woe to the earth and the sea, because the devil has gone down to you! He is filled with fury, because he knows that his time is short."

Then Satan, filled with fury, will persecute Israel. Satan is filled with great fury as he is cast to the earth because he knows that his time is short. At the end of the tribulation period he is bound during the thousand years of the millennium. At Christ's return, He will bring in his kingdom, at which time Satan will be bound for a thousand years."

"And I saw an angel coming down out of heaven, having the key to the abyss and holding in his hand a great chain. He seized the dragon, that ancient serpent, who is the devil, or Satan, and bound him for a thousand years, and threw him into the abyss, and locked and sealed it over, to keep him from deceiving the nations any more until the thousand years were ended. After that, he must be set free for a short time" (Revelation 20: 1-3).

After the thousand years, he will be released one last time to attempt a final rebellion (Revelation 20: 7-9): "When the thousand years are over, Satan will be released from his prison and will go out to deceive the nations in the four corners of the earth – Gog and Magog – to gather them for battle. In number they are like the sand of the seashore. They marched across the breadth of the earth and surrounded the camp of God's people, the city he loves. But fire came down from heaven and devoured them. And the devil, who deceived them, was thrown into the lake of burning sulfur, where the beast and false prophet had been thrown. They will be tormented day and night for ever and ever."

This will show that after the thousand years of peace and Satan's confinement, the unredeemed human heart is incurably wicked and rebellious against God. The salvation provided by Christ is the only cure for the human heart. This is why hell is eternal – because wicked natures do not change. Those who will have unwillingly conformed to the rule of Christ during the millennium will now be revealed by giving them the opportunity to rebel against Christ's rule. There must be a new birth, which they will have rejected.

Thus will end the career of the devil and his fallen angels and his warfare with God and His people: "Then I heard what sounded like a great multitude, like the roar of rushing waters, and like pearls of thunder, shouting: Hallelujah! For our Lord God almighty reigns" (Revelation 19:6).

The world-system says the real problem is not with mankind but with God. God causes guilt and sin is not our real problem but the guilt that it causes. It violates our self-esteem. It resents the offer of salvation because proud mankind sees no need for it.

This is the heart of idolatry, why people invent their own gods that will serve them, a man-centered religion of self-worship. Humanism is the result – God exists to serve mankind. The world (Satanic-system) is the organized expression of the fallen, self-centered, human race. The world-system pressures us to develop the natural man, to make this world so much of our concern that the next world takes up little thought.

"As for you, you were dead in your transgressions and sins, in which you used to live when you followed the ways of the world and of the ruler of the kingdom of the air, the spirit who is now at work in those who are disobedient" (Ephesians 2:1-2). Three times Jesus calls Satan "the prince of this world" (John 12:31, 14:30, 16:11).

The Bible warns, "do not be conformed any longer to the pattern of this world, but be transformed by the renewing of your mind" (Romans 12:2). Here we are told that we are not to allow the world to "conform us" (literally to "squeeze us into its mold"). James 4:4 tells us, "You adulterous people, don't you know that friendship with the world (Satanic-system) is hatred toward God? Anyone who chooses to be a friend of the world becomes an enemy of God?" Because believers are no longer part of the world and belong to Christ, friendship with the world-system is spiritual adultery.

In two passages, we are told of God's love for the world. One is John 3:16: "For God so loved the world that he gave His one and only Son, that whosoever believes in Him shall not perish but have eternal life." The other is 1 John 4:9: "This is how God showed His love among us: He sent His one and only Son into the world that we might live through Him."

Some see a contradiction between these two passages and I John 2:15-17: "Do not love the world (cosmos) or anything in the world. If anyone loves the world, the love of the Father is not in him. For everything in the world – the cravings of sinful man, the lust of the eyes and the boasting of what he has and does – comes not from the Father but from the world. The world and its desires pass away, but the man who does the will of God lives forever."

The difference here is that God's love is for the world of humanity apart from its Satanic-system out of which the believer has been saved. While the world, which the believer is to hate, is not the world of humanity, which we are to love and are called to bring to Christ.

The believer is not called upon to hate nature which was created by God, but the evil world-system that hates God and is hopelessly at war with God. The cosmos is characterized by its anti-God character and holds those who are "of the world" under the delusion of Satan's deception. Jesus came into our darkness and found us stumbling around, groping our way to hell. Jesus emphasized this darkness when He said, "I have come into the world as a light, so that no one who believes in me should stay in darkness" (John 12:46).

And this is why the Holy Spirit came to "convict the world of guilt" (John 16:8). But there is a point where God gives them up after repeated warnings. Three times in the first chapter of the book of Romans, we read that God gave them over to their sinful desires (verses 24, 26, and 29).

Jesus protects His people from Satan: "you, dear children, are from God and you have overcome them, because the One who is in you is greater than the one who is in the world (cosmos)" (I John 4:4). "And we know that we are the children of God, and that the whole world (cosmos) is under the control of the evil one" (I John 5:19. The believer has been "rescued from the present evil age (Galatians 1:4). And "from the dominion of darkness and brought us into His kingdom" (Colossians 1:13). And therefore are no longer to "be conformed to the pattern of this world" (Rom. 12:2).

In His High Priestly prayer, Jesus twice says believers are not of this world just as He is not of this world (cosmos)" (John 17: 14, 16). "If you belonged to the world it would love you as its own. As it is, you do not belong to the world, but I have chosen you out of the world; that is why the world hates you" (John 15:18-19).

"Don't be surprised, my brothers, if the world hates you" (John 3: 13). Believers have no relation to this fallen world. The world system is ruled by the demonic kingdom who is unified under Satan with a single goal – to disrupt God's creation.

CHAPTER 11
THE FLESH

Just as the word *world* has a physical and a spiritual meaning – to the natural physical world and the Satanic-system under the control of Satan, the word *flesh* also has a physical and a spiritual meaning – to the natural physical body and to the sin-nature we have from the fall. It is fallen human nature that has been twisted and distorted from what God intended.

Ephesians 2:3 gives a description of the workings of the flesh: "All of us also lived among them at one time gratifying the cravings of our sinful nature and following its desires and thoughts. Like the rest, we were by nature the objects of wrath." This is a description of believers before they were born again by the Holy Spirit.

When the Bible speaks of the flesh it is referring to the sin-nature. The believer in Christ is born of the Spirit and has a new nature; however the old nature still remains and these two natures struggle against each other. This is the warfare referred to in verse 8. It is referred to as the *flesh* or *sinful nature* and describes the urge to put ourselves on the throne of our lives. To put what we want above what God wants. It is this tendency that makes us sinners.

Referring to fleshly and worldly ambition, James 3:15 says, "Such wisdom does not come down from heaven but is earthly, unspiritual, of the devil," who tempts to sin. He makes his appeal through the carnal nature that we inherited from Adam and through the lure of the world-system (James 4:4). Satan seeks to ruin the effectiveness of God's people, and while Jesus' present ministry of intercession gives us the assurance that the believer's faith will not fail completely, their testimonies can be ruined. Satan's ultimate goal for all God's people is that their testimonies become ineffective.

Many times believers are disappointed by God, and we can become overwhelmed with the thought that if God really loved us He would have prevented something that has marred our lives, and we feel betrayed. Nothing hurts worse than the feeling of betrayal by a loved one, in this case the feeling that God abandoned us when we really needed Him. We can feel our faith shaken to its foundation when God acts differently than we think He should. It is hard to reconcile God's love for us when He allows so many bad things to happen to us.

Some believers have stepped out in faith expecting to see God's approval by everything working out, problems solved, and maybe even a miracle or two. But when none of these happen, they began to doubt and refuse to step out again. And through the pain and disappointment, they no longer believe that God has a plan or purpose for their lives. They have made up their minds that they will never step out in faith again. They will just give up and sit on the sidelines. They tried their best and were rejected. They feel confused and betrayed.

GOD'S WORD – THE BIBLE

At such times, we open ourselves to Satan's wiles. Somewhere along the way, we have fallen victim to the devil's schemes; and he is having a field day with us. We have allowed him to clog our lifeline to God with doubt. We must fall back on God's Word. The Bible tells us plainly that we live the Christian life by faith not feelings. Our feelings are fragile, especially when we feel betrayed by someone we thought loved us.

There are many things that we will not understand in this life because God wants us to trust Him in the dark. But we will understand fully when we enter His presence, as we are told in First Corinthians 13:12: "Now we see but a poor reflection as in a mirror: then we shall see face to face. Now I know in part; then I shall know fully, even as I am fully known." When this was written, mirrors were made of polished brass and gave a poor reflection. We are all but finite servants of God who know only in part and we are called to trust God in the dark for, "We live by faith, not by sight."

Satan's flaming arrows are designed to give us a false view of God and tempt us to doubt His Word. His foundational attack is on the Word of God. If our view of God's Word is wrong, everything is in confusion. The Bible is the foundation on which we as believers stand. If our footing is on the Word of God, we cannot be moved though heaven and earth pass away. In Mark 13:31, Jesus tells us, "Heaven and earth will pass away, but my words will never pass away." Nothing is as dependable as God's Word; it is the only sure foundation. "When the foundations are being destroyed, what can the righteous do?" (Psalms 11:3).

From the very beginning, Satan's attack has been on God's Word (Genesis 3:1-4). Peter's failure to walk on the water is given as an example to us. He was doing great until he took his eyes off of Jesus. This lesson is designed to teach us that as we go through our storms, we must keep our faith focused on Jesus. Satan is always ready to take advantage of us throughout our lives with the purpose of taking our eyes off the Lord and focusing them on ourselves and our problems. Once he gets us to take our eyes off Jesus, we will begin to be overwhelmed and sink under his attacks.

Faith is simply our response to God's promises. Faith is the key to appropriating the things of God. Faith is our response to God's ability to keep His promises. It is not the amount of our faith but the object of our faith that gives faith its power. Faith the size of a mustard seed can move mountains. Faith in itself has no power. The power is in God, and faith is the hand that receives what God provides

CHAPTER 12
THE GOOD ANGELS

The term ANGEL OF THE LORD is used many times in the Old Testament and refers to appearances of Christ in the form of an angel in connection with the divine manifestation to man on the earth. And is not to be confused with mere created angels (Genesis 18:1; 32:24-32; 48:15-16; Joshua 5:13-15; Judges 13:19-22; Psalm 34:7).

The spiritual world consists of both good and evil angels. Hebrews 1:14, referring to the good angels, says: "Are not all angels ministering spirits sent to serve those who will inherit salvation?"

From the dawn of human history, angels have manifested their presence in the world. God placed angelic guards called Cherubim in the Garden of Eden to drive out the fallen Adam and Eve and bar mankind from returning to Eden: "A flaming sword flashing back and forth to guard the way to the tree of life" (Genesis 3: 24 NIV).

In Exodus 25:17-20, God commanded Moses to have furniture made for the tabernacle, including two golden images of Cherubim. Between these two Cherubim, God would meet with him and give him His commands.

Angels are used by God to deliver messages and minister to God's people. They are from another dimension and can slip in and out of our dimension in an instant. They rejoice with us over sinners coming to Christ: "Concerning this salvation, the prophets, who spoke of the grace that was to come to you, searched intently and with the greatest care, trying to find out the time and circumstances to which the Spirit of Christ was pointing when He predicted the sufferings of Christ and the glories that would follow.

"It was revealed to them that they were not serving themselves but you when they spoke of the things that have now been told you by those who have preached the gospel to you by the Holy Spirit from heaven, even angels long to look into these things" (I Peter 1:10-12).

Scripture gives many examples of angelic protection to underscore God's use of angels. Angels are not subject to the laws of matter. They can go through physical obstacles. In Acts 12:5-11, the church was praying for Peter who was in prison waiting to be executed. While Peter was sleeping chained between two guards with Roman sentries standing guard at the entrance, an angel came into his cell through the iron bars. He woke Peter up and his chains fell off his wrists and the angel led him past the first and second guards and to the main iron gate which opened by itself; and the angel led him out to the street.

In II Kings, the Assyrian army was encamped outside the walls of Jerusalem, and the commander of the Assyrian army sent a letter to king Hezekiah telling him not to be deceived into thinking that his God could prevent Jerusalem from being conquered by Assyria. Hezekiah went into the temple and spread the letter out before the Lord and prayed that God would deliver them from the dreaded Assyrian army outside the walls of Jerusalem. God sent a massage through the prophet Isaiah that the Assyrian army would not enter Jerusalem, for God would defend the city. "That night the Angel of the Lord went out and put to death a hundred and eighty thousand men in the Assyrian camp. When the people got up the next morning – there were all the dead bodies. So Sennacherib, king of Assyria, broke camp and withdrew. He returned to Nineveh and stayed there" (II Kings 19:35-36).

Elisha and his servant were surrounded by overwhelming enemy forces (II Kings 6:14). When Elisha's servant got up the next morning and saw the city surrounded with an army of horses and chariots, he said to Elisha: "O my Lord what shall we do?"

Elisha said, "Don't be afraid, those who are with us are more than those who are with them. And Elisha prayed that his servant's eyes would be opened and his servant looked and saw the hills full of angels with horses and chariots of fire" (II Kings 6:15-17).

We are told in Psalm 34:7, "The angel of the Lord encamps around those who fear him, and he delivers them."

Psalm 91:11 says, "For He will command His angels concerning you and guard you in all your ways."

When Jezebel was trying to have Elijah killed, he was cared for by an angel (1 Kings 19: 1-9).

Daniel was protected while in the lion's den and could say, "My God sent His angel, and He shut the mouths of the lions. They have not hurt me" (Daniel 6:22).

Angels carry God's children to heaven (Luke 16:22). "The time came when the beggar died and the angel's carried him to Abraham's side." Here Jesus draws aside the curtain separating this world from the next to show that angels are active in bringing the children of God from this world to heaven.

CHERUBIM

The Cherubim are identified with the living creatures (Ezekiel 1-10: Revelation 4:6-8; 5:11,14; 7:11) and are related to the Seraphim. And like the Seraphim, they are a mysterious order of exalted angelic spirit beings closely related to the throne of God and His holiness; and they would lead in His worship and praise. Each has six wings

(Revelation 4: 8, 11). Lucifer was of this order before he fell from his high estate (Ezekiel 28:14).

SERAPHIM

They are referred to only in Isaiah 6:1-7: "In the year that king Uzziah died, I saw the Lord seated on a throne, high and exalted, and the train of His robe filled the temple. Above Him were two Seraphs, each with six wings: with two wings they covered their faces, with two they covered their feet, and with two they were flying. And they were calling to one another: 'Holy, holy, holy is the Lord Almighty; the whole earth is full of His glory'" (Isaiah 6:1-3).

They had three sets of wings: with two they covered their faces from God's holiness, and with two they covered their feet in humility, and two were for flying. They were above the throne and were calling to each other in praise to Him who sat on the throne, "Holy, holy, holy is the Lord Almighty; the whole earth is full of His glory." Like the Cherubim they had six wings (Revelation 4: 8).

MICHAEL THE ARCHANGEL

Only two names of the holy angels are given – Michael the Archangel and Gabriel. Michael, whose name means *who is like God* seems to be the only archangel, since he is always referred to with the definite article "THE Archangel. According to Daniel 12:1, he is called "The great prince who protects your people" (Israel).

In Daniel 10, Daniel sees a vision of great importance. He prays for the interpretation of the vision. He fasted and prayed for three weeks, and on the 24th day an angel came with the answer saying: "Do not be afraid Daniel. Since the first day that you set your mind to gain understanding and to humble yourself before your God, your words were heard, and I have come in response to them. But the prince of the Persian kingdom resisted me twenty-one days. Then Michael, one of the chief princes, came to help me, because I was detained there with the prince of Persia. Now I have come to explain to you what will happen to your people in the future, for the vision concerns a time yet to come" (verses 12-14).

The prince of Persia was a powerful demon assigned to the kingdom of Persia, the world power at that time, and in control of the nation of Israel. He was there to influence the Persian king to persecute Israel.

Then this unknown angel says that Michael came to help him. Michael is the angel assigned to protect Israel. Michael's help enabled this angel to come and give Daniel this message, but soon he would have to return and continue to battle with the prince of Persia and then to fight the prince of Greece because Greece was about to defeat Persia and be the new rulers over Israel (verses 20-21).

At the rapture of believers, Jesus will descend from heaven with a shout of command that the dead be raised and the living will be changed. He will be accompanied by Michael the archangel (I Thessalonians 4:16).

Michael will stand up for Israel during the tribulation period (Daniel 12:1), during which time he will fight against Satan and cast him out of the second heaven (the stellar heavens) to the earth (Revelation 12:7-9). He disputes with Satan over the dead body of Moses in Jude 9. And he gives the cry of victory at the rapture of the church (I Thessalonians 4:16).

GABRIEL

His name means *the mighty one of God* or *Champion of God*. He explains the vision of the battle of the ram and goat in Daniel 8:16 and the vision of the 70 weeks in Daniel 9:21. He announces the birth of John the Baptist (Luke 1:19) and the birth of Jesus (Luke 1:26). He gives assurance to Joseph concerning Mary's virginity (Matthew 1:20) and warns Joseph of Herod's plot to kill Jesus (Matthew 2:13) and tells him about Herod's death (Matthew 2:19).

There are unnamed angels who proclaims the birth of Christ to the shepherds in Luke 2: 9 and who encourages and strengthens Christ in His struggle in the Garden of Gethsemane (Luke 22:43) and who rolls away the stone from the tomb at the resurrection (Matthew 28:2).

An angel frees the apostles from prison in Acts 5:19, sends Philip to the desert road that goes from Jerusalem to Gaza to meet and witness to an Ethiopian Eunuch (Acts 8:26), tells Cornelius to send for Peter (Acts 10: 3), frees Peter from prison (Acts 12:7), and strikes down Herod for blasphemy (and he was eaten by worms) (Acts 12:23).

They are referred to as the heavenly host (Luke 2:13), so their normal dwelling place is in the heavens.

They were there at creation: "Where were you when I laid the earth's foundation? Tell me, if you understand. Who marked off its dimensions? Surely you know! Who stretched a measuring line across it? On what were its footings set, or who laid its cornerstone – while the morning stars sang together and all the angels shouted for joy?" (Job 38: 4-7).

They were there when the Law of Moses was given and are referenced in Hebrews 2:2-3 where the giving of the law of Moses is compared to the preaching of the gospel in Hebrews 2:2-3: "For if the message spoken by angels was binding (the Law), and every violation and disobedience received its just punishment, how shall we escape if we ignore such a great salvation (preached in the gospel)."

They were there at the birth of Christ: "And there were shepherds living out in the fields nearby, keeping watch over their flocks at night. An angel of the Lord appeared to them, and the glory of the Lord shone around them, and they were terrified. But the angel said to them, 'Do not be afraid, I bring you good news of great joy that will be for all people. Today in the town of David a Savior has been born to you; He is Christ the Lord. This will be a sign to you: you will find a baby wrapped in cloths and lying in a manger.' Suddenly a great company of the heavenly host appeared with the angel praising God and saying, 'Glory to God in the highest, and on earth peace to men on whom His favor rests'" (Luke 2: 10-14).

They were at His temptation by the devil (Matthew 4:1-10), after which we read, "Then the devil left Him, and angels came and attended Him" (Verse 11).

They were with Him during His struggle in the Garden of Gethsemane during which we read, "An angel from heaven appeared to Him and strengthened Him"(Luke 22:43).

They were at His resurrection. We read in Matthew 28: 2, "There was a violent earthquake, for an angel of the Lord came down from heaven, and going to the tomb, rolled back the stone and sat on it. His appearance was like lightning, and his clothes were white as snow. The guards were so afraid of him that they shook and became like dead men."

They were at His ascension into heaven: "After He said this He was taken up before their very eyes. And a cloud hid Him from their sight." They were looking intently up into the sky as He was going, "when suddenly two men dressed in white stood beside them, 'Men of Galilee' they said, 'why do you stand here looking into the sky? This same Jesus, who has been taken from you into heaven, will come back in the same way you have seen Him go into heaven'" (Acts 1:10-11).

And they will appear with Him at His return to the earth: "They will see the Son of Man coming on the clouds of the sky with power and great glory. And He will send His angels with a loud trumpet call, and they will gather His elect from the four winds, from one end of the heavens to the other."

"When the Son of Man comes in his glory, and all the angels with him, he will sit on his throne in heavenly glory" (Matthew 25:31).

They will be in the eternal state: "But you have come to Mount Zion, to the heavenly Jerusalem, the city of the living God. You have come to thousands upon thousands of angels in joyful assembly, to the church of the firstborn, whose names are written in heaven" (Hebrews 12: 22-23).

For all eternity, humans and angels will be companions. Believers will be attended to by the holy angels in "the heavenly Jerusalem, the city of the living God. You have come to thousands upon thousands of angels in joyful assembly" (Heb. 12: 22).

Unbelievers will also spend eternity with angels: "Depart from me, you who are cursed, into the eternal fire prepared for the devil and his angels" (Matthew 25:41).

Someday it will be over and it will be recorded of some "They overcame him by the blood of the lamb and by the word of their testimony; they did not love their lives so much as the shrink from death" (Revelation 12:11).

The great issue of life is not how much money we make or how much of a name we make for ourselves. Above all, the great issue will be, when we come to the end of our lives, whether we can say that we overcame by the blood of the Lamb and by the word of our testimony, for we loved our lives not unto death.

CHAPTER 13
PRAYER

"O You who hear prayer, to you all men will come" (Psalm 65:2).

"I call on you, O God, for you will answer me; Give ear and answer my prayer" (Psalm 17:6).

How often in Scripture we are invited to call upon the Lord and are assured that He hears and will answer our prayers. Throughout the Bible, His people have called upon Him in every conceivable circumstance and have rejoiced in the fact that He hears and answers prayer. He is not distant from His people and we need not fear because, "God is our refuge and strength, an ever present help in trouble" (Psalm 46:1).

None of His people should be troubled and fretful and weighed down with the cares of this world. We are not left to our own resources. We are not orphans but have a Father in heaven who loves us and is concerned about us and who has unlimited resources. He loves to give good things to His children.

He assures us that He is a God who delights to answer our prayers. It is His very nature to answer prayer. All the teachings of Scripture on prayer are designed to encourage us to pray. He created us to be dependent upon Him, and He is glorified when we acknowledge this dependence. He loved us enough to send the Lord Jesus to die for our sins and is already predisposed to answer us when we come to Him with our needs. He encourages us to, "Call upon Me in the day of trouble; I will deliver you, and you will honor me" (Psalm 50:15).

He tells us to come without fear or hesitation. "Therefore since we have a great high priest who has gone through the heavens, Jesus the Son of God, let us hold firmly to the faith we profess. For we do not have a high priest who is unable to sympathize with our weaknesses, but we have one who has been tempted in every way, just as we are – yet was without sin. Let us then approach the throne of grace with confidence, so that we may receive mercy and find grace to help us in our time of need" (Hebrews 4:14-16).

We are exhorted: "Do not be anxious about anything, but in everything, by prayer and petition, with thanksgiving, present your requests to God. And the peace of God, which transcends all understanding, will guard your hearts and your minds in Christ Jesus" (Philippians 4:6-7).

God forbids us to worry because it shows our lack of trust in Him. Prayer is God's answer to worry. When we dwell upon our problems, our hearts and minds become seriously affected. This becomes Satan's point of attack. When we place everything into God's hands by prayer and praise, He will keep watch over our hearts and minds.

The words "Do not be anxious about anything" refers to anxious, distressing worry, the anxiety that turns our stomachs into knots and paralyzes us with fear, not concern about our problems and needs, which should always lead us to pray. God recognizes that there are problems of legitimate concern, and we are to bring these to Him in trusting childlike faith.

It is one thing to forbid worry, but we need a solid reason why we should not worry. Here we are given the reason. God loves us and has promised to care of our needs and has provided the way. He does this in answer to trusting prayer. Not whining and complaining, but prayer, asking for His help, which He longs to give us.

"In everything by prayer and petition, with thanksgiving." The emphasis is on "everything." This defines the extent of our prayer life. It is not only the big problems but the small ones as well. Most of our lives are made up of many small problems that, if we allow them to, can overcome us. If we are going to be all that God wants us to be, we must be men and women of prayer.

Anxieties come when we see our problems as too big to overcome and indeed threaten to overcome us. God wants us to see Him as greater than all our problems. Our problems are like Goliath. When we look at our problems they seem like giants and we become overwhelmed. But when we look at God, as David did, the giants in our lives seem very small. True faith is simply a matter of perspective.

The solution to worry is trusting prayer. Faith counts on God's Word, that He will take our burdens. We are not trying to get God to assume an obligation that is rightfully not His but ours; rather we are letting Him handle an obligation that He claims as His own. Doubt says God cannot or will not assume these for us. Faith lays hold upon God to do what he has promised to do. The result of such prayer is peace.

It has been said that there are 365 "Fear nots" in the Bible, one for each day of the year. But that is wrong. If there are 365 "Fear nots" in the Bible, then we have 365 for each day. All God's promises are ours every day. We read when God led Israel out of Egypt and the supplies they brought with them ran out, He provided water from a rock and manna from the sky. For 40 years God faithfully supplied the needs for over two-and-one-half million people. There was no human source of supply. They were shut up to demonstrate God's faithfulness. The Bible tells us these events were recorded for our benefit. Their God is also our God.

God can be counted on because He has proven Himself in the past and had it recorded in the Scriptures for our benefit.

We read in Psalm 46:1, "God is our refuge and strength, an ever-present help in trouble."

"Cast all your anxiety on Him because He cares for you" (I Pet. 5:7). The word here for "cast" means a definite act of the will in committing to Him our worries. Giving them completely up to Him because we are allowing Him to assume responsibility for our welfare.

Psalm 55: 22: "Cast your cares on the Lord and He will sustain you."

We were not designed to carry heavy burdens. We were designed to depend upon God. The Bible never anticipates that we will not have troubles and trials. Rather, we are clearly told that we cannot avoid them. "Man is born to trouble as surely as sparks fly upward."

Psalm 55:22: "Cast your cares on the Lord and He will sustain you," pictures a man walking down the road carrying a heavy weight. His knees are bowed. The strain is crushing him. When he has reached the limit of his endurance, the Lord tells him to roll his burden on Him.

Many of us are like the man walking down the side of the road carrying a heavy load. A man comes along in a pick-up and offers the person a ride. The man gets in the back and sits down still carrying the heavy load on his shoulder. The driver tells him to put his burden down and rest, but the man replies, "No I'll keep carrying it. It is enough to have you give me a ride without expecting you to carry my burden too!"

There will be joy and power in our lives when we learn to bring all our needs and cares to God in prayer. Believers who do not consistently spend time in prayer have little desire to serve God and are characterized by fear and worry. The self-sufficient believer will always be a defeated thankless believer.

We should be in a constant attitude of prayer. Luther wrote, "As it is the business of tailors to mend clothes and cobblers to mend shoes, so it is the business of Christians to pray." Every believer who wants to be used of God must spend time with God and let God search his heart and deal with him. We are to bring all our needs, spiritual and physical, to Him daily in prayer.

Through prayer we can help others and share in their work. Paul was always aware of this. He exhorted believers to pray for him and his work of spreading the gospel: "I urge you, brothers, by the Lord Jesus Christ and by the love of the Spirit, to join me in my struggle by praying to God for me" (Romans 15:30).

"And pray in the Spirit on all occasions with all kinds of prayers and requests. With this in mind, be alert and always keep on praying for all the saints. Pray also for me, that whenever I open my mouth, words may be given to me so that I will fearlessly make known the mystery of the gospel, for which I am an ambassador in chains. Pray that I may proclaim it fearlessly, as I should" (Ephesians 6: 18-19).

"Devote yourselves to prayer, being watchful and thankful. And pray for us too, that God may open a door for our message, so that we may proclaim the mystery of Christ, for which I am in chains. Pray that I may proclaim it clearly, as I should" (Colossians 4: 2-4).

"Finally, brothers, pray for us that the message of the Lord may spread rapidly and be honored, just as it was with you" (II Thessalonians 3:1).

Prayer is an indispensable weapon in spiritual warfare. As believers, we are to pray for workers in the gospel. As Jesus looked upon the multitudes as ripened fields of grain perishing for lack of laborers, He said to His disciples, "The harvest is plentiful, but the laborers are few. Ask the Lord of the harvest, therefore, to send out workers into His harvest field" (Luke 10:2).

We are also to bring our unsaved loved ones and those around us to the Lord in prayer and seek for power to win them. This is the harvest field the Lord has entrusted to us. We are to pray for our fellow Christians that they may be enabled to win those around them, and we are to pray for and support financially the various soul-winning ministries that God has laid upon our hearts. We are responsible for reaching the lost by our prayers, witnessing, and financial giving.

In short, because of our frailties and proneness to sin, our responsibility to reach the lost, and our need of the power of the Holy Spirit, and because of our daily needs and our proneness to worry, we are to pray without ceasing.

Not only do we need special periods set aside during the day for prayer, but we need to be in an attitude of trusting dependence throughout the day for God's power and provisions. Without this constant, daily, systematic prayer, our lives will not have the peace and joy and fruit and victory that God wants to give us. Prayer was not ordained by God to be a mere ritual but a means of getting the things necessary for our Christian lives and work.

In Matthew 6:9-13, our Lord gives us a model prayer, the general principles about prayer. But before he does, he warns about hypocrisy and unreality in our praying.

"And when you pray, do not be like the hypocrites, for they love to pray standing in the synagogues and upon the street corners to be seen by men. I tell you the truth, they have received their reward in full. But when you pray, go into your room, close the door, and pray to your Father, who is unseen. Then your Father, who sees what is done in secret, will reward you. And when you pray, do not keep babbling like pagans, for they think they will be heard because of their many words. Do not be like them for your Father knows what you need before you ask Him."

Jesus is warning about irreverence in prayer. Play acting – going through the motions with no real approach to God. Their motive for praying was "to be honored by men," to be praised as pious and devout. The Pharisees prayed much but they were hypocrites. They were professional prayers, play actors, devoid of sincerity. A hypocrite was an actor putting on a performance before men, not real prayer. In Psalm 145:18 we read, "The Lord is near all who call upon Him, to all who call upon Him in truth." The words *in truth* mean *in reality* or *sincerity*. Prayer performed merely as a *duty* is not prayer.

Jesus says in verse 6, "But when you pray." Here the emphasis is on the word YOU, in contrast to the hypocrites who want to be seen by men; YOU are to go to your room and close the door and pray. This could refer to any secret place, even to one's own heart and mind. Jesus is not prohibiting public prayer. The point is that our attention is to be on God not on what men think. The hypocrites who only want men's praise will get what they bargained for; that's all they will get! But we are to approach God in sincerity with our prayers, and He will answer us. We are not to practice ritual praying using many repetitions like the pagans.

"This, then, is how you should pray"(verse 9). Note that He does not say "WHAT" you should pray, but "HOW" you should pray. This is a model or pattern prayer, a guideline for prayer.

"This, then, is how you should pray:

'Our Father in heaven,
hallowed be your name,
your kingdom come,

> your will be done on earth as it is in heaven.
> Give us today our daily bread.
> Forgive us our debts,
> As we have forgiven our debtors.
> And lead us not into temptation,
> but deliver us from the evil one.

'For if you forgive men when they sin against you, your heavenly Father will also forgive you. But if you do not forgive men their sins, your Father will not forgive your sins'" (Matthew 6:9-13).

"Our Father in heaven." This is the basis for praying. As believers, God is our Father and we are His Children. Out of His goodness, God has answered prayers of those who are not His children. But He has made no promise to do so, except for the prayer of repentance and faith in Christ for salvation. The promise to consistently answer prayer is given to His children. This is the natural outgrowth of His relationship to us as Father. It should be the most natural thing for believers to go to their heavenly Father for all our wants and needs. He is already predisposed to hear the cry of His children. As the words "Our Father" is a reference to our intimate and personal relationship to Him and our love for Him, the words "in heaven" are at the same time a reference to His holiness and majesty and the awe and reverence we have for His greatness. This constitutes true worship.

"Hallowed be your name." God's name represents all that He is. We are to bow our hearts before Him who is more than we can ever imagine or dream. This is a request that He will be held in adoration and devotion in our lives and universally among men and women. As believers, we are not only to reverence Him with our lips but with our lives, as we seek to make Him known to others through the gospel.

"Your kingdom come, your will be done on earth as it is in heaven." This refers to Christ's climatic second coming with His kingdom. But until then it is the rule of God in the hearts of men and women through faith in Christ. His kingdom is on earth today, in that His people are members of His kingdom in *mystery* or *secret* form: "For he has rescued us from the dominion of darkness and brought us into the kingdom of the Son He loved" (Colossians 1:13).

Believers today are members of that kingdom. This is what Jesus meant when He said, "But seek first His kingdom and His righteousness, and all these things will be given to you as well" (Matthew 6:33).

He is not simply saying that we should be saved ourselves, but that those who are saved should seek to advance the rule of God in the hearts of men now, and thus prepare them for the literal, visible kingdom of Christ when He returns. For as Jesus told Nicodemus, without the new birth men cannot see the kingdom of God.

We are to submit ourselves to do the will of God and seek to bring others into that will. To do the will of God is the highest attainment of men or angels.

"Give us today our daily bread." Bread here refers to our daily needs. Here we are taught to live one day at a time, and trust God for that day's physical necessities. We do not have to hoard for the future, though God does expect us to plan ahead and prepare for the future. But we do not have to fret and worry about the future. We can trust God for each day's needs and rest in His care.

"Forgive us our debts as we also have forgiven our debtors." In Matthew 6:14-15 Jesus said, "For if you forgive men when they sin against you, your Heavenly Father will also forgive you. But if you do not forgive men their sins, your Father will not forgive your sins."

This forgiveness has to do with our relationship as members of His family. The believer in Christ is forgiven once-for-all as far as salvation is concerned. But we still need daily forgiveness as far as our communion or fellowship with God is concerned.

Jesus illustrated this in John 13:6-10. Jesus was washing His disciples feet when He came to Peter, Peter protested, "You shall never wash my feet." Jesus answered "unless I wash you, you have no part with me." To which Peter replied, "Then Lord, not just my feet but my hands and my head as well!" Jesus answered: "A person who has had a bath needs only to wash his feet."

Jesus makes a distinction between the whole body being bathed and washing the feet. Here bathing refers to the "washing of rebirth" (Titus 3:5). All believers are washed and clean as far as salvation is concerned. But we live in a polluted and defiled world, and we need daily cleansing from walking in this dirty world, illustrated by Jesus washing the disciples feet. Without this daily cleansing, Jesus said we would "have no part with Him." This refers to our fellowship with Him.

While our relationship to Him as His children cannot be broken, our fellowship with Him can be broken. This concerns our family relationship. Just as a child can displease his father and it will not affect his relationship as his child, it may disrupt his fellowship until he restores fellowship by removing what had broken their fellowship. This implies that we confess our sins and seek His forgiveness.

"And lead us not into temptation, but deliver us from the evil one." This is a petition that God, through His providence, will guard us from situations that will become a snare of the devil. Of course, we ourselves can create these situations. But if we honestly seek to please God, He will providentially keep us from the evil one. He will keep us from temptations above what we can stand.

This is the pattern prayer that the Lord gave us, and it covers every area of our lives and service generally. The Bible has much to say about prayer. A very important part of prayer is thanksgiving. How many of us are negligent of expressing gratitude for the many blessing that we have already received from God. We should be just as definite in returning thanks as we are in asking. We should be continually filled with thanksgiving and praise.

We should all pray that God will give us just a glimpse of who He is and the love He has for us, as we are told in Psalm 118:1, "Give thanks to the Lord, for He is good; His love endures forever."

We are exhorted in Hebrews 13:15, "Through Jesus, therefore, lets us continually offer to God a sacrifice of praise – the fruit of lips that confess His name."

In Luke 17:11-19, we have the account of the ten lepers whom Jesus healed. He told them to go to the priests to receive the certificate required by the law of Moses to show that they had been cleansed of leprosy. On the way they were suddenly cleansed, all ten of them. Only one of them, however, went back to Jesus and fell down at His feet, thanking Him: "One of them, when he saw he was healed, came back, praising God in a loud voice. He threw himself at Jesus' feet and thanked Him." Disappointed, Jesus asked, "Were not all ten cleansed? Where are the other nine?"

If we will be consistent in returning thanks for blessings received, it will keep before us how often our prayers are answered and will greatly increase our faith for asking other things of God.

Prayer is vital for Christian service. Those who live lives of little prayer will never accomplish much for God, no matter how busy they are for Him. The Holy Spirit never fills people of little prayer. Without the empowering of the Holy Spirit, we can accomplish nothing no matter how talented and gifted we are. Prayer will bring direction and power into our lives. Of course, prayer cannot be separate from Bible study. Bible study will breathe life into our prayers, and prayer in turn will breathe life into our Bible study. They are like two gears perfectly fitted into each other, and each turns upon the other.

Even a casual study of the gospels reveals these two factors permeated the life of our Lord. How often we find Him quoting the Scriptures and revealing their deeper meaning. How He read and loved the Scriptures! He said, "Man shall not live by bread alone, but by every word that comes from the mouth of God."

Our Lord's earthly life was also saturated with prayer. He so completely renounced the independent use of His divine power and prerogatives that He depended upon His Father for everything. He was like any of His followers, except He was without sin. His power and needs were supplied by His Father just as ours must be.

He would rise long before sunrise to prayer (Mark 1:35). It was in prayer that He received directions for the day. After a very busy day in Capernaum, He rose the next morning before daylight for directions for that day and received them. His disciples found Him and said: "Everyone is looking for you." But He had already received the will of the Father, and said to them, "Let us go somewhere else – so I can preach there also" (Mark 1:37-38).

Often He would find a secluded place and spend the whole night in prayer (Luke 6:12). His life was extremely busy and under constant pressure. He often did not even have time for meals (Mark 6:31). But He would always take time for prayer, often sacrificing much needed sleep.

At His baptism by John, beginning His public ministry, we find Him praying, "When all the people were being baptized, Jesus was being baptized too. And as He was praying, heaven was opened and the Holy Spirit descended upon Him in bodily form like a dove. And a voice came from heaven: 'You are my Son, whom I love; with you I am well pleased.'" What happened while He was praying indicates what He was praying for. From this we learn that the Lord Jesus was praying for the Holy Spirit's power for His ministry.

His ministry was maintained by prayer: "Yet the news about him spread all the more, so that crowds of people came to hear him and to be healed of their sicknesses. But Jesus often withdrew to lonely places and prayed" (Luke 5:15-16).

It was following prayer that He did His great miracles:

Walking on the water (Matthew 14:23-33). The feeding of the four thousand (Matthew 15:36). The healing of the demon possessed boy (Mark 9:14-29). The feeding of the five thousand (John 6:11). The raising of Lazarus (John 11:41-42), and was undoubtedly true of all His miracles.

Before choosing His twelve Apostles He spent the night in prayer: "One of those days Jesus went out to a mountainside to pray, and spent the night praying to God. When morning came, He called His disciples to Him and chose twelve of them, whom he also designated apostles" (Luke 6:12-13). In a special sense, these men would carry on His work after His ascension and would write much of the New Testament.

It was after prayer that He put the crucial question to His disciples: "Who do you say I am?"(Luke 9:18-21). It was while on the mount in prayer that He was transfigured (Luke 9:28-31).

He told Peter, "Simon, Simon, Satan has asked to sift you as wheat. But I have prayed for you, Simon, that your faith may not fail" (Luke 22:31-32). In John 17:20-26 we have Jesus' great High Priestly prayer in which He made petitions for Himself, His disciples, and all who would believe on Him.

The final hours before His arrest and trial were spent in prayer (John 17: 20-26). He prayed while on the cross. And now at the right hand of the Father, He continues to pray: "Therefore He is able to save completely those who come to God through Him, because He always lives to intercede for them" (Hebrews 7:25).

Jesus is our great example in everything. Let us learn from the great emphasis He put on the Scriptures and prayer. He never taught His disciples how to preach or run a church or how to raise money, but He taught them how to pray.

It is recorded that all the great people of the Bible were men and women of prayer. Abraham prayed and Lot was delivered (Genesis 19:29). Jacob prayed and his name was changed to Israel, "prince with God" (Genesis 32:24-28). Barren Hannah prayed for a son and Samuel was born (I Samuel 1:11,20). Samson prayed and his strength was restored and he gained his greatest victory over the enemies of Israel (Judges 16:28).

Elijah prayed and won a great victory over the prophets of Baal (I Kings 18:25-40). Elisha prayed and was given a double portion of Elijah's power (II Kings 2:9). Nehemiah prayed and God moved upon the heart of the heathen king of Persia to give permission to the Jews of the captivity to return to their land and rebuild the city of Jerusalem, and also to provide the resources for the task.

Zachariah and his barren wife Elizabeth prayed for a child and John the Baptist was born (Luke 1:13). The early church prayed in the face of persecution for boldness and were filled with the Holy Spirit (Acts 4:31). Peter prayed and Dorcus was raised from the dead (9:40-41). The Church prayed and Peter was delivered from prison (Acts

12:5-10). Paul prayed and brought forth churches throughout the Roman world.

These are but a few of the prayers that brought forth great things for the glory of God. These were men and women just like us who knew their weakness and cried to God, whose strength was made perfect in their weakness. Under every conceivable situation, God has met the needs of His praying people. From the splitting of seas (Exodus 14:15-25) to the feeding of men by angels (I Kings 14:15-25) and ravens (I Kings 17:2-7), He has shown Himself to be "an ever present help in trouble" (Psalm 46:1).

The history of the church outside the Bible reveals the same thing: The race is not to swift, nor the battle to the strong, but to those who learn to wait upon God. For the most part, these were men and women of average intelligence, talents and abilities, some of them far below average. But through prayer, they were changed into men and women who accomplished great things for God.

For instance, we all thrill to read of the great revivals of John and Charles Wesley, but God knows that without a humble woman, Susanna Wesley, their mother, who daily prayed over her children and took time from her toils to "bring them up in the training and instruction of the Lord" (Ephesians 6:4), we would never have heard of her famous sons.

Prayer brings power into our lives, and it is not only full time Christian workers who need this power. All believers need this power to raise their families and win their loved ones for Christ. We are just as responsible in our sphere of influence as they are in theirs. Because of the power of prayer, there is no telling the influence of a humble housewife or bed-ridden child of God.

The simple Bible-believing, praying Christian is a mighty instrument in the hand of God, as an insignificant jawbone of an ass was used by Samson to slay a thousand men. It was not the strong, seasoned warrior Saul that God used to bring down the giant Goliath but the seemingly insignificant young shepherd boy, who learned to meditate on the word of God and pray while tending his flocks.

"For the weapons of our warfare are not carnal, but mighty through God to the pulling down of strongholds" (II Corinthians 10:4). The word "carnal" here means "human." Though believers are merely human, they do war with human weapons. We read of believers' need for special power because of their supernatural enemy in Ephesians 6:10-13. Here we are told that our warfare is against the satanic forces of darkness that influence the affairs of men.

Ephesians 6:14-17 lists this armor. Then in verse 18 we note the intensity, "With this in mind, be alert and always keep on praying for all the saints." God wants His people to be armed and dangerous, not negotiating or bargaining with the enemy. He wants them to be in a death struggle without the option of retreat until the enemy is defeated.

So often we are like the Israelites as they entered the land of Canaan. God told them to go in and drive out the enemy and subdue the land. They were to go in His power and drive out the enemy. But after driving the enemy out of certain areas and settling in them, they became comfortable and instead of finishing the war they were content to co-exist with the enemy, allowing them to keep their strongholds because the battle would be difficult and they had settled down in their comfort zone.

As a result, they were plagued by these enemies throughout their history. So often we become content with being saved and settle down and try to keep from making waves that might stir up the enemy and cause us to have to give up our comfort. But the picture we have here in Ephesians is constant warfare, so that, "You may be able to stand your ground, and after you have done everything, to stand" (Ephesians 6:13). After driving off the enemy, we are not to sit down and rest, but remain standing, ready for the next attack to come.

In order to pray correctly, we must pray in the Biblical sense. Prayer is not some magical ritual. It is not like rubbing a genie's lamp. Prayer has no inherent power in itself. Its power lies in its ability to move God in our behalf. Prayer was established by God as a natural outgrowth of our relationship to Him as our Father. It is asking and receiving from God what He wants to give to His children.

It is not a lever to move God to do what He does not want to do, but it is holding our hands out to receive what He wants to give us. He has given us conditions that must be met. He will not give us simply anything we ask for; no good and loving father would be so gullible. But He has set conditions for answered prayer. These are not conditions that will earn answers to our prayers, but rather they clear the way for a holy God to give us the best things He has for us.

One condition that God has laid down in His Word is that we pray according to His will. "This is the confidence we have in approaching God: that if we ask anything according to His will, He hears us. And if we know that He hears us – whatever we ask – we know that we will have what we asked of Him" (I John 5:14-15).

The conditions that God makes are not hard, difficult conditions but conditions that every child of God should gladly seek to meet. No Christian should be afraid of God's will. God's will is always for our benefit and should be our greatest joy. Jesus said, "I seek not to please myself but Him who sent me" (John 5:30). The will of the Father was not some distasteful thing that He forced himself to do, but it was the very thing He sought and loved to do.

Now we are told that if we pray according to God's will, whatever we ask for we will receive. The will of God is not hard to know. It is clearly revealed in His Word. If there are some specific areas of His will for particular individuals not clearly revealed in the Bible, these will be made clear to us as we live according to what HAS been revealed in the Scriptures.

For instance, we know from the Word of God that it is His will that all believers seek to win others to Christ; but it is not clearly revealed that God wants so and so to be a pastor, evangelist, missionary, or some other full-time Christian service. This is the will of God for certain individuals. This will be revealed to them as they obey the general will of God to win souls.

Then too, we are told that it is God's will that we give to support the preaching of the gospel; but we are not told specifically where to give. This will be clearly revealed if we are willing to obey the general command to give.

The Scriptures are full of promises. These promises are also a revelation of God's will. These are to be claimed and received by prayer. It is essential that we know the Word of God if we are to pray in the will of God. As we study His Word, we will be amazed at how extensively He has made His will known. Anything that you desire that you think would please God to give, that would honor Him, you should pray for with confidence, and this requires knowledge of the Bible.

If, while praying, God does not lead us to pray differently, then we have every reason to expect the answer to that prayer. At times we may pray for things that are good and proper, but God may have something better for us and sets us praying in that direction.

This is illustrated by the prayer life of Paul referred to in II Corinthians 12:7-9: "To keep me from becoming conceited because of these surpassingly great revelations, there was given to me a thorn in the flesh, a messenger of Satan, to torment me. Three times I pleaded with the Lord to take it away from me. But He said to me 'my grace is sufficient for you, for my power is made perfect in weakness.' Therefore I will boast all the more gladly about my weaknesses, so that Christ's power may rest upon me."

Paul was afflicted by some "thorn in the flesh." He took it to God in prayer. God told Paul that He had something better for him and turned Paul's prayer in that direction. God knew that Paul wanted more than anything else to win others to Christ. So God told Paul that it would be better to leave the thorn because through his weakness Paul would depend all the more on God, and through Paul's weakness God's strength would be made perfect, which would result in Paul being more effective in winning others to Christ. Paul's reaction was that he would gladly keep the thorn that the power of Christ may rest upon him.

God must reserve the right to correct our prayers because we do not see the whole picture as He does.

Another condition for having our prayers answered is praying in Jesus name. We are told in John 15:16, "You did not choose me, but I chose you and appointed you to go and bear fruit – fruit that will last. Then the Father will give you whatever you ask in my name."

And John 16: 23-24: "In that day you will no longer ask me anything. I tell you the truth, my Father will give you whatever you ask in my name. Until now you have not asked for anything in my name. Ask and you will receive, and your joy will be complete."

When we use another person's name, we use His authority as his representative. To pray in Jesus name is to pray in His authority. But He will only endorse the things He approves of. They must be consistent with His character and interests. This presupposes the surrender of our interests for His. We cannot use His name for things that He would not approve of, but only for the things He wants us to have. It does not mean that we simply say at the end of our prayer "in Jesus name." Our requests and motives will determine if it is really in His name.

Then we are to pray in the Holy Spirit, "Praying always with all prayer and supplication in the Spirit" (Ephesians 6:18), "We do not know what we ought to pray for, but the Spirit Himself intercedes for us with groans that words cannot express. And He who searches our hearts knows the mind of the Spirit, because the Spirit intercedes for the saints in accordance with God's will" (Romans 8:26-27).

Prayer is essential to the Christian life, and we should expect the Holy Spirit to be intimately involved. The Holy Spirit urges us to pray and guides us according to Scripture that He inspired, as to what we should pray for, and then energizes those prayers.

In order to pray in the Spirit, we must be in fellowship with Him. Not grieving Him, nor quenching Him. We are commanded in Ephesians 4:30: "And do not grieve the Holy Spirit, with whom you were sealed for the day of redemption." We grieve the Holy Spirit when we do what He does not want us to do.

Then we are told in I Thessalonians 5:19, "Do not put out the Spirit's fire." We quench the Holy Spirit when we put off or don't do what He wants us to do. We must not break fellowship with Him by grieving Him or quenching Him if we are going to pray effectively. Without this our prayers will be weak and barren.

In order to pray in the Holy Spirit, we must study and meditate much on the Scriptures which He inspired. As we do this, the Spirit will illuminate our understanding to pray as we should.

Another condition for effective praying is to pray in faith. In Mark 11:22, Jesus said "have faith in God." This is important to remember. Our faith is to be in God Himself. Often we have more faith in our problems than in God. Another mistake we often make is to focus on our faith, analyzing it to see if it feels strong enough. When we look at our faith, our hearts sink, but when we look to God, our faith grows.

True faith begins where our fears end. Conflict is part of faith. This conflict arises because the fear of our situation arouses in us hopelessness. True faith overcomes doubt. This is why God oftentimes allows situations to come into our lives where all the outward circumstances are contrary to faith. True faith trusts God in spite all the circumstances being contrary to faith. When Peter got out of the boat and walked on the water in Matthew 14:22-33, it was a battle between faith in Jesus and faith in the huge waves.

Referring to unbelief, Hebrews 12:1 commands us "let us throw off everything that hinders and the sin that so easily entangles." Chapter 11 shows this sin to be unbelief. This is the great crippler of the believer's life: "And without faith it is impossible to please God" (Hebrews 11:6).

Hebrews 11:1 gives us the definition of faith: "now faith is being sure of what we hope for and certain of what we do not see." Faith is assurance or confidence that God will do what we ask of Him. In Matthew 21:22 Jesus said, "If you believe, you will receive whatever you ask for in prayer."

God wants us to have a bold faith, and it must be remembered that real faith is always based on something. It is not some magical thing that we can use to get what will not please God. Faith must be based upon the Word of God, His promises or upon the nature of God. Faith without a basis is merely make-believe and has no more substance than a puff of smoke.

But if it is based upon God's Word, then it is as sure as God Himself. That is why Hebrews 4:16 says, "Let us approach the throne of grace with confidence, so that we may receive mercy and find grace to help in our time of need." This refers to a bold, confident approach to the very throne of God where we know we will find a gracious, sympathizing Father.

Faith does not look at the circumstances but to the promises of God. Faith is trust in God's faithfulness. We're not to make the mistake of looking at our faith to determine if it is strong enough. We are to look at God's faithfulness and trustworthiness, and faith will take care of itself.

Another condition for answered prayer is abiding in Christ. "If you remain in me and my words remain in you, ask whatever you wish, and it will be given you" (John 15:7). This refers to fellowship, not salvation. We are united to Christ positionally, based solely on what Christ did in our behalf, and this never changes or varies. But our fellowship within His family can be broken.

We abide in Christ in communion by allowing His Word to abide in us, to continue to have its way in our lives. We are to study His Word, meditate upon it, and obey it. We are told in Proverbs 28:9, "If anyone turns a deaf ear to the law, even his prayers are detestable." God will treat our prayers as we treat His Word. As we feed upon His Word, we will begin to think His thoughts and want the things he wants. His will becomes our will.

If we abide in Christ, we will be obedient. "We have confidence before God and receive anything we ask because we obey His commands and do what pleases Him" (I John 3:22). God cannot condone sin in the lives of His people and will withhold what He otherwise wants to give us, until we deal with our sins and confess them. To abide in Christ, we must put away all known sin in our lives: "Surely the arm of the Lord is not too short to save, nor His ear too dull to hear. But your iniquities have separated you from your God. Your sins have hidden His face from you, that He will not hear" (Isaiah 59:1-2).

When our iniquities come between us and God, He will not hear us. We are told in Psalm 66:18, "If I had cherished sin in my heart, the lord would not have listened; but God has surely listened and heard my voice in prayer" (Psalm 66:18-19). We must ever be on guard against sin in our lives. Sin will paralyze our spiritual lives and our prayers will go unanswered.

We cannot be at peace with our sins and at peace with God. "He who conceals his sins does not prosper, but whoever confesses and renounces them finds mercy" (Psalm 28:13). We cannot hold on to known sin and abide in Christ. We must not make excuses for our sins but loathe them as leprosy or cancer. Sin in our lives is like Achan in the camp of Israel; it brings shame and defeat (Joshua 7:24-26).

If we abide in Christ we will not pray with wrong motives: "When you ask you do not receive, because you ask with wrong motives, that you may spend what you get on your pleasures" (James 4:3). It is not only the prayer itself that God considers, but the motive behind it.

If we abide in Christ and His Word abides in us, our prayers will be for His glory. Love for Him will motivate all our prayers and everything we do. We will not have resentment or bitterness toward others: "And when you stand praying, if you hold anything against anyone, forgive him, so the your Father in heaven may forgive you your sins"(Mark 11:25-26).

This forgiveness by God concerns our fellowship, not our salvation – it is forgiveness within the family of God. As children of God, we have already been forgiven once and for all as far as our salvation is concerned. This concerns fellowship with God as our Father. As far as our fellowship is concerned, God cannot allow certain things in the lives of His children and remain in fellowship.

In order to have our prayers answered, we must be in fellowship with God, which is the meaning of abiding in Christ. If we break this fellowship, we cannot pray effectively until we are forgiven and fellowship is restored. But God will not forgive us if we fail to forgive others. And our fellowship with Him will remain broken, and our prayers will be hindered.

If God were to answer our prayers while we remained unforgiving and bitter toward others, He would appear to condone this attitude. By refusing to answer our prayers, He shines a spotlight on our sin until we put it away.

We are not only to forgive those who have wronged us, but we are to seek reconciliation with those WE have wronged: "Therefore if you are offering your gift at the altar and there remember that your brother has something against you, leave your gift there in front of the altar. First go and be reconciled to your brother; then come and offer your gift" (Matthew 5:23-24).

If we are abiding in Christ, we will not be selfish with our material possessions. "If a man shuts his ears to the cry of the poor, he too will cry out and not be answered" (Proverbs 21:13). God is loving and gracious. He is concerned about the poor and He expects His people to be also. If we do not have compassion on the cry of the poor, God will not hear us when we pray. He cannot condone callousness to those who are in need. He is greatly saddened when His children selfishly hoard their material possessions when so many are in need.

We are also to give to God's work. "Remember this: Whoever sows sparingly will also reap sparingly, and whoever sows generously will also reap generously. Each man should give what he has decided in his heart to give, not reluctantly or under compulsion, for God loves a cheerful giver" (II Corinthians 9:6-7).

As children of God, saved by the blood of Christ, we should be extremely concerned that others hear this saving gospel of Christ. All believers are responsible to support those who faithfully preach the gospel.

Now these conditions that we have been considering are not really many conditions. They are really one condition. If we abide in Christ and His Word abides in us, we will want the things He wants us to have. If His Word is abiding in us, having its way in our lives, then we are abiding in Christ. And if His Word abides in us, then we will pray in faith, for faith comes from hearing the Word of God.

Faith must have something to believe. This is found in God's Word. The Holy Spirit works through the Word that He inspired or breathed out. If we abide in Christ we can pray in His name, representing His interests. This is the same as praying in the Holy Spirit who will only lead us to pray for things we can ask in Jesus name – for His interests. Jesus said, "But when He, the Spirit of truth comes, He will guide you into all truth . . . He will bring glory to me by taking from what is Mine and making it known to you" (John 16:13-14).

The Holy Spirit will only lead us to pray for things in the will of God: ". . . the Spirit intercedes for the saints in accordance with God's will" (Romans 8:27).

When these conditions are met, Jesus tells us to persevere until we receive the answer. "Then Jesus told His disciples a parable to show them that they should always pray and not give up. He said, 'in a certain town there was a judge who neither feared God nor cared about men. And there was a widow in that town who kept coming to Him with the plea, 'Grant me justice against my adversary.'

"For some time he refused. But finally said to himself, 'Even though I don't fear God or care about men, yet because this widow keeps bothering me, I will see that she gets justice, so that she won't eventually wear me out with her coming!'

"And the Lord said, 'Listen to what the unjust judge says, and will not God bring about justice for His chosen ones, who cry to Him day and night? Will He keep putting them off? I tell you, He will see that they get justice, and quickly" (Luke 18:1-8).

Here Jesus used an illustration to increase our faith. If the unjust judge, who cares nothing for God or man, would answer the widow because of her persevering. How much confidence can we have that God, who loves us, will give us what we ask.

Many times God will give us our requests very soon. Sometimes He gives assurance that He has heard us and gives us peace about the matter until the answer comes. But at other times we must dig in and persevere in wrestling or struggling in prayer. Paul referred to this type of praying as a struggle: "I urge you, brothers, by our Lord Jesus Christ and by the love of the Spirit, to join me in my struggle by praying to God for me" (Romans 15:30).

In the Old Testament it is illustrated by Jacob, who said to the Angel of the Lord after wrestling with Him all night, "I will not let you go unless you bless me" (Genesis 32:26).

Actually the delay is on our part, not God's. Often much has to be accomplished in us before we are prepared to receive our request and we must allow God time to deal with us. Sometimes we must persevere in prayer and heart searching, confessing our sins and putting them away, allowing God time to show us our sins and reveal His will to us and make changes in our prayers, and reveal wrong motives until we are brought to the place where He can answer our prayers. Persevering prayer is God's method of preparing His children for His greatest blessings.

FASTING

Throughout the Bible, prayer and fasting are associated with wholehearted prayer, a symbol of mourning and repentance. There are times of sorrow and defeat, grief and mourning, when we should turn from normal food and sleep and give ourselves completely to prayer and seeking God's power. When the world begins to mold us into its image and sin loses its sense of shame and guilt, it is time to fast and pray as we confess our sins and unbelief. But we are warned by the Lord Jesus against fasting as a ritual or form without sincerity. It does not put God in our debt, but it does focus our attention on things that need it most.

Let us confess our sin of prayerlessness. And let us set out to learn to pray as God would have us pray. Unanswered prayer is a tragedy. But this situation can be changed. If we will humble ourselves, repent of our sins, check our motives, and study the Scriptures and obey them, God will gladly work with us and lead us. He longs for His people to pray and longs to answer their prayers.

God is seeking our fellowship, not because He needs it, but because we need Him! He has made Himself comprehensible to our finite minds and wants us to know Him better. He will always remain mysterious, but it will be the mystery of a Father who loves His children. He is not concerned with the form of our words but with the sincerity and reverence of our hearts. The more we learn about Him, the more our faith and confidence in Him will grow, until at last we stand in the majesty and glory of His presence for all eternity.

www.ingramcontent.com/pod-product-compliance
Lightning Source LLC
Chambersburg PA
CBHW050436010526
44118CB00013B/1559